SEVEN GREAT APOLOGISTS

7 DEFENDERS OF THE FAITH
WHO IMPACTED THEIR WORLD

PHIL FERNANDES

IBD Press
Bremerton, WA

Published by IBD Press,
A ministry of the Institute of Biblical Defense

P. O. Box 3264
Bremerton, WA 98310
(360) 698-7382
instituteofbiblicaldefense.com

ISBN: 978-0-615-58763-9

Contents

Foreword

....

There is a story I remember about the late Walter Martin, the Original Bible Answer Man. He used to teach a Bible study at his church, and people did not give much thought as to who it was teaching them. To many, he was just Walter. I relay this story because we sometimes forget or take for granted those teachers who we know personally; sometimes we do not appreciate just how much these people have influenced us.

This leads me to Dr. Phil Fernandes. I have known Phil for about twenty years, and two things that have always impressed me about him are his love for our Savior, the LORD Jesus, and his commitment to serving Him. His contributions to my life and the lives of those of Trinity Bible Fellowship, the church he pastors, and those involved with the Institute of Biblical Defense (IBD), the apologetic ministry he founded, are immeasurable.

In the years that IBD has existed, Dr. Fernandes has met and dialogued with many of the "who's who" of apologetics and has debated many of the leading atheists of our day. Phil has personally introduced us to two of the world's leading apologetic scholars: Dr. Gary Habermas and Dr. J.P. Moreland. He brought both of them up to Washington State at different times for us to sit under their teaching. In his endorsement of Phil and IBD, J.P. Moreland states that "the programs offered through IBD provide the student with a good foundation in apologetics and introduces him or her to the labor of reason."

Dr. Fernandes is a world class scholar who stays abreast of cutting edge trends in apologetics, theology, philosophy, and political thought. One of his strengths is not being shackled by the thought of one system such as evidentialism or presuppositionalism and the like. He sees the strengths of other systems without succumbing to the pressure of throwing out the entire system of thought simply because he does not agree with every tenet of an apologist's methodology. A good example is that Phil appreciates Gordon Clark's refutations of non-Christian systems of thought without holding to Clark's dogmatic presuppositionalism. This is refreshing.

The pages that make up the work of this current book give an overview of seven great apologists Norman Geisler, Gary Habermas, Gordon Clark, Cornelius Van Til, Francis Schaeffer, Walter Martin, and Blaise Pascal. They may use different approaches and methodologies, but all are major contributors to the field of apologetics. Dr. Fernandes may have not reached their level of notoriety, but those who know him personally and professionally recognize the scholarship of Dr. Fernandes. It is without hesitation and with extreme honor to write a few words about Dr. Fernandes. I highly recommend this book. Enjoy!

Gary Tronson
MA in Theological Studies
(Liberty Baptist Theological Seminary)
Pastor of Missions, Trinity Bible Fellowship
Professor of Bible & Missions, Institute of Biblical Defense

Introduction

Apologetics is the defense of the Christian faith. I have been involved in apologetics ministry for over twenty years. During this time, I have had the privilege of reading the insights of many great apologists. The seven apologists in this small book represent just a small taste of the wisdom one can find in apologetic writings. These apologists have had a great influence on the way I defend the faith. In fact, I have been blessed to meet with and study under the teachings of two of these great apologists: Norman Geisler and Gary Habermas.

Norman Geisler is a classical apologist—he defends the faith using traditioanl arguments for God's existence and historical arguments for Jesus' resurrection and deity. He is also willing to use modern scientific evidence for the existence of God. Geisler's method of defending the faith is closer to my method than that of any of the other apologists discussed in this book.

Gary Habermas is an evidentialist who uses historical evidences to argue that Jesus rose from the dead. He also argues that Jesus did in fact claim to be God, and that His resurrection proves His claims to be God to be true. Habermas may be the world's leading expert on the historical evidence for Jesus' resurrection. Over the years, I have borrowed much apologetic ammunition from Habermas for my historical defense of the faith.

Gordon Clark was a Christian philosopher who believed that everyone must presuppose or assume their first principles. From these first principles, we deduce all our other beliefs. Clark believed that the only presuppositions that adequately explain reality in a non-contradictory fashion are: 1) the existence of the Triune God, 2) His revelation in the Bible, and 3) the law of non-contradiction (what Clark called "the law of contradiction"). Clark used the law of non-contradiction to disprove non-Christian belief systems. In fact, Clark is at his best when he refutes non-Christian systems of thought. Later in his career, Clark began to argue that truth can only be found in the Scriptures. Most apologists reject Clark's "Scripturalism," realizing that God has revealed Himself in nature as well as in the Bible.

Cornelius Van Til argued that Christians should not reason like non-believers reason. For the non-believer thinks he is autonomous; he thinks he lives and thinks totally in his own power and has no need for God in his thought life. Van Til says the Christian must not argue to God. Instead, the believer must argue from God—we must presuppose God. Van Til allows for no fact to be interpreted apart from God—all facts are God created facts. Van Til believed the Christian apologist must presuppose the existence of the Triune God who has revealed Himself in Scripture. If we do not presuppose this we will never really know anything. Van Til is willing to refute the beliefs and arguments of non-believers. But, the only argument for God he allows is his own transcendental argument.

Francis Schaeffer treated the Christian world view as a hypothesis which he was willing to test. He believed that Christianity provided the best and only true explanation of the world in which we live. Schaeffer argued that the only way to explain the personality of man was to acknowledge the existence of a personal, infinite God. Schaeffer viewed reality as a puzzle, but argued that only Christisanity provides man with the missing pieces to complete the puzzle. Schaeffer had a very successful ministry reaching out to "modern" people who were looking for meaning and truth. Schaeffer emphasized speaking the truth in love.

Walter Martin was the original "Bible Answer Man." He founded the Christian Research Institute, a ministry devoted to apologetics research. Martin's apologetic ministry focused on refuting the teachings and practices of non-Christian cults. He also defended the Christian faith against the false teachings of the New Age Movement. Martin would defend the faith by turning to the Scriptures to refute the false teachings promoted by pseudo-Christian religions. With the rise of non-Christian cults and neo-pagan beliefs, the importance of comparative religious apologetics should not be overlooked.

Blaise Pascal was a seventeenth-century French mathematician and scientist. He believed that fallen man does not use his reason in an unbiased way. Pascal believed man's will and desires are more influential on man's thought than is his reason. He believed no one approaches issues such as the existence of God or the truth of Christianity in an unbiased manner. Therefore, Pascal sought to make a case that the wise man will be biased towards God before examining the evidence. Once this is established, Pascal turns to evidence for Christianity from fulfilled prophecies, miracles, and makes a historical case for the truth of the Christian faith.

It is my hope that the reader, by reading this book, will learn to enjoy the richness and diversity in some of the different apologetic methodologies. I also pray that this book will help the reader in his own defense of the faith. For, we are to *"sanctify Christ as Lord in our hearts, always being ready to make a defense of the hope that is in us, yet with gentleness and reverence"* (1 Peter 3:15).

CHAPTER ONE

The Apologetic Methodology of Norman Geisler

....

INTRODUCTION

Norman Geisler may be the leading Christian apologist of the latter half of the twentieth-century. Geisler founded the Evangelical Philosophical Society and the International Society of Christian Apologetics, and is also a former president of the Evangelical Theological Society. He has successfully debated, in defense of Christianity, some of the world's leading non-Christian thinkers.

Geisler earned his Ph.D. in philosophy at Loyola University. Over the decades, he has established himself as the leading evangelical Thomist (someone who utilizes the philosophical thought of Saint Thomas Aquinas). He has taught theology, philosophy, and apologetics at some of America's leading evangelical schools such as Dallas Theological Seminary, Trinity Evangelical Divinity School, and Liberty University. Geisler helped found Southern Evangelical Seminary (one of today's leading training grounds for Christian apologists) in North Carolina and taught apologetics and theology there. It is hard to find an evangelical apologist who has had a greater impact on the evangelical thought of his day.

Geisler is a prolific author. Some of his most notable works that deal with apologetics and his apologetic methodology are: Christian Apologetics,[1] Philosophy of Religion[2] (co-authored with Winfried Corduan), I Don't Have Enough Faith to Be an Atheist[3] (co-authored with Frank Turek), When Skeptics Ask[4] (co-authored with Ronald Brooks), and The Baker Encyclopedia of Christian Apologetics.[5] In this chapter, we will examine his apologetic methodology. First, we will look at his seminal work Christian Apologetics.

METHODOLOGY—HOW DO WE FIND TRUTH?

Geisler is one of the most thorough apologists—he begins his apologetic system asking the question: How do we find truth?[6] In an attempt to answer this question, he examines several options before identifying what he believes to be the correct method of finding truth. Once he identifies this method, he applies it to worldviews (i.e., different ways to explain reality), testing them to determine the true world view. Once he finds the true world view, he then turns to historical evidences to defend Christianity.

Geisler examines and critiques several proposed methods for finding truth. First, he looks at agnosticism.[7] Hard agnosticism is the view that man cannot know truth. Geisler shows that hard agnosticism is self-refuting, for it is a claim to know something— that man cannot know anything. But, if man can know that man cannot know, then, at least, man can know this. Hence, agnosticism fails—man can know truth. Geisler critiques the agnostic Immanuel Kant. Kant argued that we can only know reality as it appears to us, not reality as it is. However, Geisler points out that if Kant is correct, then man can know the reality that we cannot know reality—but, this is knowledge of reality. Hence, Kant's agnosticism is self-refuting. Since agnosticism fails, it is possible for man to know truth.

Second, Geisler focuses on rationalism as a test for truth.[8] Pure rationalism fails as a test for truth for several reasons. Rationalism can prove that which is false (i.e., contradictions cannot be true) and it can show what is possible; but, by itself, it is unable to prove that which is true. Also, if man can prove everything through reason alone, then we would be able to prove our first principles (i.e., our starting points) through reason alone. But, then these would not be our first principles since there would be premises that precede them. And these premises would need proof as well. Hence, pure rationalism leads to an infinite regress of premises and knowledge can never get started. Therefore, pure rationalism fails as a method to find truth.

Third, Geisler shows fideism to be an inadequate test for truth.[9] Fideism is the view that we must merely believe things without evidence for them. Applied to religion, fideists contend that we must blindly believe religious tenets without evidence. Geisler points out that fideism fails because it refuses to test truth claims—it asks us to merely believe. The fideist says we should not use reason to defend our religious beliefs, yet the fideist himself, by claiming to be a fideist, uses the law of non-contradiction (a rational principle). In essence, the fideist is using reason in an attempt to argue against reason.

Fourth, Geisler identifies the problems with using experientialism as the test for truth.[10] Geisler points out that no experience is self-interpreting—we interpret our experiences through the lenses of our world view (i.e., our view of reality). Also, there is no way to adjudicate between conflicting truth claims if experientialism is the sole test for truth. Each person would hold to their own experience, but there would be no way to prove one experience true and the other experience false.

Fifth, Geisler declares evidentialism to be an inadequate test for truth.[11] Facts do not come with their own built-in interpretations—again, they must be interpreted by the world view of the person. We interpret facts by our worldview and not the other way around. A mere appeal to facts will not settle disputes between different world views; our test for truth must be more foundational than facts.

Sixth, pragmatism also fails as a test for truth.[12] Pragmatism is the belief that whatever works is true. Geisler points out that even though all truth must ultimately work, not everything that works is true. Often, lies work—when a doctor tells a patient he is recovering when he is not may help him rehabilitate more rapidly, but it is still a lie. Just because something works does not mean it is true. Also, Geisler points out that, as finite humans, we cannot always see the long range results of a view. Sometimes what works in the short term will fail in the end. Whatever the case, pragmatism fails as a test for truth.

Seventh, Geisler rejects combinationalism as a test for truth.[13] Merely adding together inadequate ways to find truth will not produce an adequate way to find truth. Geisler illustrates this point by stating that adding leaky buckets will continue to fail to hold water. Hence, merely combining inadequate tests for truth is equivalent to a new inadequate test for truth.

After showing the limitations of these seven failed tests for truth, Geisler proposes his own tests for truth. These tests are as follows: 1) actual unaffirmability as a test for the falsity of world views, 2) actual undeniability as a test for the truth of world views, and 3) systematic consistency (a combinational test for truth statements within a particular world view).[14]

Actual unaffirmability deals with things that are impossible to affirm without contradiction. For instance, if someone says he does not exist, he must first exist in order to make the denial. Hence, my nonexistence is actually unaffirmable. Any world view that is actually unaffirmable must be false.[15]

Actual undeniability deals with truths that can only be denied with contradiction. An example of this is that it is actually undeniable that I exist; for, if I did not exist I would not be able to deny my existence. I must exist to be able to deny my existence. Hence, my existence is actually undeniable. Any world view that is actually undeniable must be true.[16]

Systematic consistency uses combinationalism, not to test the truth of a world view, but as a test for the truth of statements within a world view.[17] The three main components of Geisler's systematic consistency test are consistency, empirical adequacy, and experiential relevance. Consistency determines whether the beliefs within a world view are non-contradictory. Empirical adequacy says that a world view must explain all the relevant facts in question. If a world view is unable to explain relevant data, it is a weak world view. Experiential relevance declares that a world view must be livable. If it is not possible to live consistently with a world view, then that world view should be abandoned.[18]

Geisler uses the first two tests (actual unaffirmability, and actual undeniability) to test the main world views to determine which one is true. The world views he tests are: deism, pantheism, panentheism, atheism, and theism. Geisler argues that theism is the true world view. Once this is settled, Geisler then uses the test of systematic consistency to determine which theistic religion is true.

THEISTIC APOLOGETICS—WHICH WORLD VIEW IS TRUE?

Deism is the world view that teaches that God created the universe but does not intervene—He does not perform miracles. Deism is based on a faulty view of science in which the laws of nature cannot be violated. In reality, the laws of nature do not prescribe what must occur; they describe what generally occurs. Natural laws do not rule out the possibility of miracles. If God cared enough to create the universe (a point agreed to by Deists), then it makes sense that He would care enough to communicate with His creatures through miracles. If God is powerful enough to create the universe (also accepted by Deists), then He is powerful enough to perform miracles. Hence, if Deism is true, then God is both willing and able to perform miracles. But, then Deism would be false.[19]

Pantheism is the world view that believes that God is everything—God is the universe. God is a non-personal force. In this world view, since all reality is one being (monism), man is God. Geisler exposes the weaknesses of pantheism by showing that it fails to adequately explain the existence of the finite self and the existence of evil. Also, pantheism teaches that God is beyond reason; hence, God is unknowable. But, this creates a problem for pantheism. For, how could the pantheist know that pantheism is true if God is unknowable? If God is completely unknowable, how could we know that God is the universe and is non-personal. For these reasons, pantheism fails as a world view.[20]

Panentheism is the world view that professes belief in the existence of a God who has both a finite aspect and an infinite aspect to His basic nature. But, this is incoherent. For God cannot be both finite and infinite in His basic nature. If God has limitations in His basic nature, he would, by definition, be a finite, limited god. A changing, finite god would need to have his existence grounded by an infinite, non-changing God (i.e., the God of theism). Therefore, the panentheistic world view fails.[21]

Atheism is the world view that teaches there is no God. This world view fails for several reasons. First, Geisler shows that arguments for atheism are invalid and self-refuting. Second, atheism offers no adequate explanation for the existence of the universe, personality, intelligence, and morality. The existence of the universe, personality, intelligence, and morality provide good evidence for theism (i.e., the belief in a personal God who is both transcendent and immanent).[22]

After showing the weaknesses of the above world views, Geisler argues that the theistic world view is actually undeniable.[23] First, Geisler argues that "some things undeniably exist." For example, I must exist in order to deny my existence—I cannot consistently deny my own existence. Therefore, I undeniably exist. Second, "my nonexistence is possible." There was a time I did not exist. I depend on the existence of other things for my continued existence. Third, "Whatever has the possibility not to exist is currently caused to exist by another." Fourth, "There cannot be an infinite regress of current causes of existence," for then each cause would also be an effect. There would be no cause for the continuing existence of the entire series. Fifth, "Therefore, a first uncaused cause of my current existence exists." If this were not the case, then no finite things would now exist. Sixth, Geisler shows that "this uncaused cause must be infinite, unchanging, all-powerful, all-knowing, and all-perfect." If this were not the case, then the infinite cause of all finite existence would not really be infinite. However, an infinite uncaused cause must exist in order to ground the continuing existence of all finite things. Geisler argues that "this infinitely perfect being is appropriately called 'God,'" for there cannot be two infinite beings. Hence, God exists. This God is identical to the God of the Bible. Therefore, the God of the Bible exists.[24]

Dr. Geisler, through his argumentation, has shown that the existence of the God of theism is actually undeniable. Since all other world views contradict theism, they must be false. Only theism is the true world view.

CHRISTIAN APOLOGETICS—WHICH THEISTIC RELIGION IS TRUE?

Once Geisler proves theism to be true, he then moves on to argue that Christian theism is true, whereas Islamic theism and Jewish theism are false. Christianity, Islam, and Judaism are the three great theistic religions. Geisler turns to history to argue for the truth of Christian theism. He shows that, through the study of ancient history and by using the principle of systematic consistency, the truth of the Christian world view can be established.

First, Geisler argues that miracles are possible. If the theistic God (a personal, all-powerful God who created the world but sustains its existence) exists, then miracles are possible. Miracles cannot be ruled out a priori (before examining the evidence for particular miracle claims).[25]

Second, Geisler argues that history is objective—there is a real history independent of any particular historian's speculation about history. History is as objective as modern science since both deal with probabilities (not certainties). Hence, miracle claims must be tested.[26]

Third, Geisler argues that the truth of Christian theism can be verified through an examination of history. First, he argues for the historical reliability of the New Testament manuscripts. Second, he argues for the deity and authority of Jesus Christ. Third, he argues for the inspiration and authority of the Bible.

Geisler points to several pieces of evidence for the historical reliability of the New Testament manuscripts. He shows that the New Testament has greater manuscript evidence for its reliability than any other ancient writing. It has more copies, a smaller gap between the earliest extant copies and the original, and a higher percentage of agreement between existing ancient copies. No ancient writing comes close to the New Testament in reference to manuscript evidence.[27] By referring to archaeological confirmation, ancient secular writings, and the writings of the early church fathers, Geisler presents strong arguments for the early dates of the New Testament books, thus showing that they were written by eyewitnesses who knew Jesus (or people who knew eyewitnesses).[28]

Next, Geisler argues that Jesus did in fact claim to be God on numerous occasions. Jesus claimed to be Jehovah and equal with God. He accepted worship, taught others to pray in His name, and placed His words on the same level as the words of God.[29] Geisler argues that Jesus proved His claims to be true by rising from the dead, fulfilling numerous Old Testament messianic prophecies, and performing miracles.[30] Therefore, Jesus is God.

As God, Jesus verified that the Bible is God's Word. He taught that the Old Testament is God's Word and promised that the Holy Spirit would guide His followers into all the truth, thus producing the New Testament.[31] Since the Bible is God's Word, it is without errors—it it totally true in the original manuscripts. Hence, other religions that disagree with the Bible are false.[32]

11

GEISLER'S TWELVE STEP APOLOGETIC ARGUMENT

In more recent times, Norman Geisler has spelled out his apologetic case for Christianity, in a more simplified fashion, in a twelve step argument. This argument can be found in his work, co-authored with Frank Turek, I Don't Have Enough Faith to be an Atheist:

- Truth about reality is knowable.
- The opposite of true is false.
- It is true that the theistic God exists.
- If God exists, then miracles are possible.
- Miracles confirm a message from God.
- The New Testament is historically reliable.
- The New Testament says that Jesus claimed to be God.
- Jesus' claim to be God was miraculously confirmed by:
- His fulfillment of Old Testament prophecies.
- His sinless and miraculous life.
- His prediction and accomplishment of His resurrection.
- Therefore, Jesus is God.
- Whatever Jesus (who is God) teaches is true.
- Jesus taught that the Bible is the Word of God.
- Therefore, the Bible is God's Word and anything opposed to it is false.[33]

First, truth about reality is knowable. If someone says "there is no truth," he contradicts himself. For the statement "there is no truth" would be true. Hence, truth exists. If someone says "man cannot know truth," then this would be a truth known by man. Hence, it is also self-refuting. Therefore, truth exists and man can know it.

Second, the opposite of true is false. That which contradicts the truth must be false. If the statement "God exists" is true, then the statement "God does not exist" must be false. Contradictory statements cannot both be true.[34]

Third, it is true that the theistic God exists. Geisler now uses several arguments for God's existence. He uses two types of cosmological arguments: the argument from the beginning of the universe and the argument from the continuing existence of the universe. Geisler argues that whatever has a beginning needs a cause, and that the universe has a beginning—this is confirmed by the big bang model, the expansion of the universe, and the second law of thermodynamics. Therefore, if the universe had a beginning, it needs a cause. Geisler also argues that it is impossible for only contingent beings to exist—beings whose continued existence is dependent on the existence of other things. Eventually, we must arrive at a being that is necessary, a being that cannot not exist. This being grounds the continuing existence of everything else that exists.[35]

Geisler also uses two forms of the teleological argument for God—the argument from design.[36] The first type of design argument argues from the Anthropic Principle that universe was fine-tuned to support human life on the planet earth. This cannot be a coincidence—an intelligent Designer must have pre-planned the universe for the purpose of supporting human life on the planet earth. The second type of design argument deals with the specified and irreducible complexity of life. Even a single cell animal contains enough genetic information to fill 1,000 complete sets of Encyclopedia Britannica. That amount of highly complex information could not have come about by chance. Life—even the most basic forms of life—had to be intelligently designed.

Geisler also uses the moral argument for God's existence. Everyone appeals to an absolute standard of morality when we condemn the actions of others. But, if there exists an absolute moral law, there must exist an absolute moral Lawgiver. If there exists no universal moral law, then there is no real difference between living a life like Mother Theresa or living a life like Adolph Hitler.[37]

Fourth, if God exists, then miracles are possible. Since Geisler has already shown that the evidence indicates that the theistic God does exist, then miracles cannot be ruled out beforehand. Miracles are possible, for the theistic God is both willing and able to perform miracles. Hence, we must examine the historical evidence to determine if certain miracles have occurred.[38]

Fifth, God uses miracles to confirm a message from Him. God does not perform miracles to entertain; He performs miracles to place His stamp of approval on the message that is being proclaimed.[39]

Sixth, Geisler argues that the New Testament is historically reliable. Geisler builds a strong case that the New Testament presents early eyewitness testimony to the life, teachings, miracles, death, and resurrection of Jesus. Ancient non-Christian authors confirm what the early church believed. The New Testament has more extant copies than any other ancient writing. These copies have a far greater percentage of agreement than any other ancient writing. The gap between when the New Testament was originally written and the oldest copies we currently have is a smaller gap than that of any other ancient writing. The writings of the early church fathers show the New Testament books to be first century ad documents. This shows that the New Testament was written while the apostles (who personally knew Jesus) were still alive. Hence, the New Testament accounts were not legends that developed decades or centuries after Jesus lived; they were reliable historical accounts that accurately depicted the life and ministry of Jesus.[40]

Seventh, the New Testament (which we have shown to be authored by the generation that knew Jesus) portrays Jesus as a man who claimed to be God on numerous occasions. Hence, the earliest evidence indicates that Jesus thought of Himself as equal to God.[41]

Eighth, Jesus' claim to be God was confirmed by His fulfilling Old Testament prophecies of the coming Messiah,[42] His miraculous works, and His bodily resurrection from the dead. Geisler and Turek present numerous evidences for Jesus' bodily resurrection and refute alternative, naturalistic theories used to explain away the resurrection.[43] Therefore, Jesus is God and whatever He teaches is true (i.e., points 9 and 10 above).

Jesus taught the Old Testament is the inerrant Word of God and promised to complete God's revelation through the teachings of His apostles (i.e., the New Testament). The Holy Spirit would guide the apostles into the truth and bring to their remembrance all that Jesus taught them. Hence, Jesus (who is God) taught that the Bible is God's Word (point 11).[44]

Finally, since the Bible is God's Word, whatever it teaches is true. Whatever contradicts the Word of God must therefore be false.[45] This concludes Norman Geisler and Frank Turek's case for Christianity.

GEISLER'S SCIENTIFIC CASE FOR CREATION

Norman Geisler has also established himself as a leading scientific apologist. This section will draw heavily upon the information found in the book Origin Science by Norman L. Geisler and J. Kirby Anderson.[46]

HISTORY OF THE CREATION-EVOLUTION DEBATE

The creation model is the view that God created the universe without using evolution. The creation model dominated modern science before 1860.[47] Modern science was started by men who believed in the existence of the God of the Bible. Galileo, Isaac Newton, Francis Bacon, Johannes Kepler, and Blaise Pascal are just a few who fit into this category.[48] Their belief in God's existence formed the foundation for modern science. They believed that a reasonable God created the universe in a reasonable way, so that through reason man could find out about the universe in which he lives.[49] In other words, the universe makes sense only because God designed it to make sense. Today, however, atheistic evolutionists have rejected this base for modern science.[50] They have rejected the existence of a reasonable God. But the question that they must face is this: "Without a reasonable God, can a person really expect the universe to make sense?"

The evolution model is the view that life spontaneously evolved from non-life without intelligent intervention.[51] The evolution model dominated modern science after 1860.[52] Charles Darwin published his book The Origin of Species around that time.[53] Darwin proposed a naturalistic explanation for the origin of the universe, first life, and new life forms.[54] He taught that nature can be explained without appealing to a supernatural origin. Darwin's proposal quickly became the predominant "scientific" view.

THE SCIENTIFIC METHOD

Evolution is not a scientific fact. The scientific method consists of six steps: 1) observation, 2) proposal of a question or problem,

3) hypothesis (an educated guess), 4) experimentation, 5) theory (a hypothesis with a high degree of probability), and 6) natural law (a theory thought to be valid on a universal scale).[55] Evolution is not a scientific law or theory, let alone a scientific fact. The supposed evolutionary changes from one species to another cannot be observed.[56] They supposedly occurred in the past. Therefore, since observation is the initial step in the scientific method, evolution cannot be proven through the scientific method.

The creation view is in the same category as evolution. Creation, scientifically speaking, is not a fact, law, or theory. Like evolution, the supposed creation is a singular event in the past. It cannot be observed. Therefore, both creation and evolution are only scientific models; they represent different ways to interpret the same evidence.[57]

This does not mean that creation and evolution cannot claim to be scientific. Contrary to popular belief, the scientific method is not the only way to search for truth in the field of science. Forensic science (crime scene investigation) does not use the scientific method, for the crime can no longer be observed. Still, forensic science is a legitimate science.[58] Science can be separated into two main divisions: operation science and origin science. Operation science deals with the repeatable; it is science of the observable present. It uses the scientific method. Forensic science, creation, and evolution do not fall into this category.[59] Origin science, on the other hand, deals with the non-repeatable; it deals with the singular events of the past. Origin science does not utilize the scientific method since singular events of the past can no longer be observed.[60] Forensic science, creation science, and evolutionary science fall into this category.

ORIGIN SCIENCE

Since the non-repeatable events of the past cannot be observed, origin science does not make use of the scientific method. Instead, origin science uses the principles of analogy (also called uniformity) and causality to determine whether or not a model is plausible.[61] The principle of analogy states that when a scientist observes a cause bringing about a certain effect in the present, he should posit the same kind of cause for a similar effect in the past.[62] In other words, similar effects usually have similar causes. The principle of causality states that every event must have an adequate cause.[63] A scientist should use these two principles to determine the plausibility (or lack of plausibility) of a particular model.

Since the creation model and the evolution model fall under the heading of origin science, the principles of analogy and uniformity must be applied to them to determine which model is more plausible. It must be understood that the creation model and the evolution model both deal with the same evidence. An example of this is common anatomy. Common anatomy deals with the similarities in the body parts of different species. Examples of common anatomy are the similarities that exist concerning the arm of a man, the arm of an ape, the wing of a bird, and the fin of a shark. Both creationists and evolutionists agree to the common anatomy between different species of animal life. However, the two models interpret the evidence differently. The evolution model teaches that common anatomy proves common ancestry.[64] Common ancestry is the view that all species are related since one species has evolved into another. The creation model teaches that the same data (common anatomy) proves the existence of a common Designer. Animals often share common anatomy due to their being created and designed by the same God.[65]

Which model is more plausible? In order to answer this question, the principles of analogy and causality must be applied to the origin of the universe, the origin of first life, and the origin of new life forms. Both the creation model and the evolution model must be tested in these three areas to ascertain which model is more plausible.

THE ORIGIN OF THE UNIVERSE

Did the universe have a beginning, or did it always exist? This is a very important question. For if the universe had a beginning, it would need a cause. It could not have evolved into existence from nothing. If the universe is eternal then it may not need a cause. Fortunately, science is not silent on this question. The second law of thermodynamics is called energy deterioration. This law says that the amount of usable energy in the universe is running down.[66]

Eventually, all the energy in the universe will be used up. This means that the universe is winding down. If it is winding down, it had to have been "wound up." If the universe is going to have an end, it had to have a beginning. There had to be a time when all the energy in the universe was usable; this marks the beginning of the universe.

The expansion of the universe and the big bang model also confirm the beginning of the universe.[67] In 1929, astronomer Edwin Hubble discovered that the universe is expanding at the same rate in all directions.[68] As time moves forward the universe is growing apart. This means that if one went back in time the universe would get denser. If one goes back in time far enough, the entire universe would be contained in what scientists have called "a point of infinite density."[69] But, a point can only be finitely dense. For a point to be infinitely dense it would have to be non-existent. Therefore, the universe came into existence from nothing a finite time ago.

There have been two main attempts to refute the proposition that the universe had a beginning. The first is the steady-state model. This view holds that the universe had no beginning. Instead, it always existed in the same state. However, because of the mounting evidence for the big bang model, this view has been abandoned by most of its adherents.[70]

The second attempt to evade the beginning of the universe is called the oscillating model. This model teaches that, at some point during the universe's expansion, gravity will halt the expansion and pull everything back together again. From that point there will be another big bang. This process will be repeated over and over again throughout all eternity. However, the oscillating model fails for three reasons. First, there is no known principle of physics that would reverse the expansion of the universe into another big bang. Second, current scientific research has shown that the universe is not dense enough for gravity to pull it back together again. Third, even if one could prove that several big bangs have occurred, the second law of thermodynamics would still require that there was a first big bang.[71]

Therefore, science has shown that the universe had a beginning, but, since from nothing, nothing comes, something must have caused the universe to come into existence. Everything that has a beginning needs a cause. Since the universe needs a cause, the creation model is more plausible than the evolution model. If the universe were eternal, then the evolution model could claim some type of plausibility. But, for the above reasons, this is not the case. The universe is not eternal; it had a beginning. Something separate from the universe had to cause it to come into existence.

THE ORIGIN OF FIRST LIFE

Evolution teaches spontaneous generation—that life came from non-life without intelligent intervention.[72] However, spontaneous generation violates the law of biogenesis and the cell theory. The law of biogenesis states that "all living things arise only from other living things."[73] The cell theory defines the cell as the most basic unit of life, and declares that "new cells arise only from pre-existing cells."[74] Both the law of biogenesis and the cell theory are accepted by evolutionists; the evolutionists merely assume that first life is the exception to these principles. But, a model that violates scientific theories and laws should be abandoned. This is especially true when there is a rival model that does not violate scientific theories and laws.

The creation model posits the existence of an intelligent Being in order to bridge the gap from non-life to life. The creation model recognizes that the specified complexity (highly complex information) found in a single-celled animal could not be produced by chance. A single-celled animal has enough genetic information to fill one volume of an encyclopedia.[75] Just as an explosion in a print shop cannot randomly produce one volume of an encyclopedia, there is no way that a single-celled animal could have been produced by mere chance. Intelligent intervention was needed.[76]

Natural laws by themselves do not produce specified complexity. Geisler illustrates this point by stating that though natural laws can explain the Grand Canyon, they cannot explain the faces on Mount Rushmore.[77] The faces on Mount Rushmore reveal evidence of intelligent design.

Evolutionists often offer the Miller and Urey experiments as evidence that life has been produced from non-life in the laboratory. In response, several things should be noted. First, Chandra Wickramasinghe, one of Britain's most eminent scientists, calls these experiments "cheating." Miller and Urey start with amino acids, break them down, and then recover them. They do not produce something that wasn't there to begin with.[78] Second, Geisler states that the Miller and Urey experiments do not produce life. They only produce amino acids, which are the building blocks of life. Amino acids are to life what a single sentence is to one volume of encyclopedia.[79] Third, Geisler points out that even if these experiments did produce life from non-life in the laboratory (which they don't), it would support the creation model, not the evolution model. The reason for this is clear. The experiments would merely prove that to get life from non-life intelligent intervention (i.e., the scientists) is needed. The experiments would not prove that life spontaneously arose from non-life.[80]

Therefore, the creation model is more plausible than the evolution model when explaining the origin of first life. Intelligent intervention is necessary to produce life from non-life. It could not have happened by accident.

THE ORIGIN OF NEW LIFE FORMS

Many people believe that the fossil record proves evolution, but, this is not the case. In the fossil record, new life forms appear suddenly and fully developed.[81] There is no evidence of transitional forms (missing links). There are no fins or wings becoming arms. There are no intermediate forms. The gaps between forms in the fossil record are evidence against evolution, not for evolution.

Evolution teaches that single-celled animals eventually evolved into human beings. Of course, evolutionists claim this took long periods of time to be accomplished. A single-celled animal contains enough information to fill one volume of encyclopedia,[82] but the human brain contains enough information to fill twenty million volumes of encyclopedia.[83] Natural law, no matter how much time is involved, can never produce twenty million volumes of encyclopedia from one volume. Intelligent intervention is needed to produce more complex information.[84]

Evolutionists often point to mutations as the process by which evolution takes place.[85] However, mutations do not add more complex information to the genetic code. Instead, they merely garble the already existing genetic code.[86] For evolution to take place, new genetic information is needed. For example, single-celled animals would need new genes for the development of teeth, yet mutations produce no new genetic information.[87]

Simple life forms do not go to complex life forms through natural law alone.[88] Time plus chance plus natural laws can never produce more complex information.[89] Something must impart more information. Therefore, the creation model is more plausible than the evolution model concerning the origin of new life forms.

CONCLUSION OF GEISLER'S SCIENTIFIC CASE FOR GOD

The scientific case for creation is very strong. Though it is true that creationists have never seen the invisible Creator, evolutionists also have never seen the supposed evolutionary changes of the past. The principles of analogy and causality support creationism as a superior model to evolution. Blind chance and natural laws are inadequate causes for the origin of the universe, first life, and new life forms. An intelligent Cause is needed in each case. The cause of the beginning of nature cannot be nature itself. No being can preexist its own existence in order to cause its own existence. Therefore, nature needs a supernatural Cause. This supernatural Cause must be an intelligent Being to bring life from non-life and complex life forms from simple life forms. Hence, the creation model is more plausible than the evolution model.

CONCLUSION

Dr. Geisler's apologetic methodology is a thorough, consistent type of classical apologetics. Geisler is indebted to the philosophy of Thomas Aquinas—his apologetic system is Thomistic.

There are three main steps in his defense of Christianity. First, he identifies the appropriate tests for truth—a step ignored by most apologists. Second, he proves the existence of the theistic God with actual undeniability. And third, he shows Christianity to be true with a high degree of probability. (Historical events of the past can only be proven with probability.)

Geisler uses other evidences for the Christian faith besides philosophical and historical evidences. He is willing to utilize scientific apologetics in his defense of the faith. Refusing to put

God's truth in a pre-determined "box," he is willing to use evidence for God wherever that evidence is found.

Norman Geisler's apologetic methodology should serve as a model for other apologists. He deals with important issues often ignored by most apologists (i.e., the concept of truth, finding proper tests for truth, the objectivity of history, the possibility of miracles, etc.). Though Geisler's apologetic methodology is somewhat complex, he was willing to simplify it and break it down for Christian lay people in order to assist them in their defense of the faith. Geisler's apologetic methodology has established him as one of the foremost Christian apologists of the twentieth and early twenty-first centuries. One cannot consider oneself knowledgeable in contemporary apologetics without reading the apologetic works of Norman Geisler. Even if a Christian apologist chooses to use a different methodology to defend the Christian faith, he does a disservice to himself if he chooses to ignore the contribution Norman Geisler has made to the history of Christian thought and the evidences and arguments he has developed. Geisler laments that contemporary evangelicals have ignored the work of Thomas Aquinas.[90] It would also be unfortunate if evangelicals choose to neglect the thought of Dr. Geisler.

ENDNOTES
1. Norman L. Geisler, Christian Apologetics (Grand Rapids: Baker Book House, 1976).

2. Norman L. Geisler and Winfried Corduan, Philosophy of Religion, 2nd ed. (Grand Rapids: Baker Book House, 1988).

3. Norman L. Geisler and Frank Turek, I Don't Have Enough Faith to be an Atheist (Wheaton: Crossway Books, 2004).

4. Norman L. Geisler anzd Ron Brooks, When Skeptics Ask: A Handbook on Christian Evidences (Wheaton: Victor Books, 1990).

5. Norman L. Geisler, Baker Encyclopedia of Christian Apologetics (Grand Rapids: Baker Book House, 1999).

6. Geisler, Christian Apologetics, 11-147.

7. Ibid., 13-27.

8. Ibid., 29-46.

9. Ibid., 47-64.

10. Ibid., 65-81.

11. Ibid., 83-99.

12. Ibid., 101-116.

13. Ibid., 117-132.

14. Ibid., 133-147.

15. Ibid., 141-143.

16. Ibid., 143-145.

17. Ibid., 145-147.

18. Ibid., 147.

19. Ibid., 151-171.

20. Ibid., 173-192.

21. Ibid., 193-213.

22. Ibid., 215-235.

23. Ibid., 237-259.

24. Ibid., 238-250.

25. Ibid., 263-283.

26. Ibid., 285-304.

27. Ibid., 305-308.

28. Ibid., 308-327.

29. Ibid., 330-334.

30. Ibid., 339-351.

31. Ibid., 353-376.

32. 376-377.

33. Geisler and Turek, I Don't Have Enough Faith to be an Atheist, 33.

34. Ibid., 35-69.

35. Ibid., 73-94.

36. Ibid., 95-167.

37. Ibid., 169-193.

38. Ibid., 197-217.

39. Ibid., 216-217.

40. Ibid., 221-297.

41. Ibid., 327-354.

42. Ibid., 329-336.

43. Ibid., 299-320.

44. Ibid., 355-376.

45. Ibid., 375.

46. Norman L. Geisler and J. Kirby Anderson, Origin Science (Grand Rapids: Baker Book House, 1987),
entire book.

47. Ibid., 37-52.

48. Ibid.

49. Ibid., 37-40, 51.

50. Ibid., 52.

51. Ibid., 82-86.

52. Ibid.

53. Ibid.

54. Ibid.

55. Tom M. Graham, Biology, the Essential Principles (Philadelphia: Saunders College Publishing, 1982), 6.

56. Geisler and Anderson, 15.

57. Ibid.

58. Ibid., 25.

59. Ibid., 36.

60. Ibid., 127-132.

61. Ibid.

62. Ibid., 131-132.

63. Ibid., 130-131.

64. Morris, Many Infallible Proofs (El Cajon, California: Master Books, 1974), 252-255.

65. Ibid.

66. Graham, 75.

67. William Lane Craig, Apologetics: An Introduction (Chicago: Moody Press, 1984), 81-83.

68. Ibid., 82.

69. Ibid.

70. Ibid., 83.

71. Ibid., 83-88.

72. Morris, Many Infallible Proofs, 260.

73. Graham, 18.

74. Ibid., 12.

75. Geisler and Anderson, 162.

76. Ibid., 162-163.

77. Ibid., 141.

78. Varghese, Roy Abraham, The Intellectuals Speak Out About God (Dallas: Lewis and Stanley, 1984), 34.

79. Geisler and Corduan, 105-106.

80. Geisler and Anderson, 138-139.

81. Ibid., 150-152.

82. Ibid., 162.

83. Ibid.

84. Ibid., 163.

85. Morris, Many Infallible Proofs, 256.

86. Ibid.

87. Charles Caldwell Ryrie, You Mean the Bible Teaches That . . . (Chicago: Moody Press, 1974), 111.

88. Geisler and Anderson, 150.

89. Scott M. Huse, The Collapse of Evolution (Grand Rapids: Baker Book House, 1983), 94.

90. See Norman L. Geisler, Thomas Aquinas: An Evangelical Appraisal (Grand Rapids: Baker Book House, 1991).

CHAPTER TWO:

The Historical Apologetics
of Gary Habermas

Gary Habermas is the distinguished professor of philosophy and theology at Liberty University. Many consider him to be the world's leading expert on the historical evidence for Jesus' resurrection from the dead. Habermas provides historical evidence to show that Jesus really did claim to be God and that He physically rose from the dead. Jesus' resurrection from the dead in history provides strong proof for the truth of His claim to be God incarnate.

THE APOSTOLIC FATHERS: EVIDENCE FOR JESUS

Habermas finds evidence for the historical Jesus in numerous ancient sources. The primary evidence Habermas utilizes to build his case for Jesus is the core data, found in the New Testament, which is accepted as historical by the vast majority of New Testament critical scholars today. Still, Habermas is willing to use ancient extra-biblical sources to find evidence for the true Jesus of history. These sources include the writings of the apostolic fathers, other early Christian literature, and ancient secular writings.

The apostolic fathers were leaders in the early church who personally knew the apostles and their doctrine.[1] Most of their writings were produced between 95 and 150AD.[2] There were also other prominent Christian thinkers who wrote about Jesus during this time period.

Radical New Testament scholars have attempted to find the so-called true Jesus of history, but it was their goal to find a non-supernatural Jesus who never claimed to be God. These scholars believe that Christ's claim to be God and Savior, and His miraculous life (especially His bodily resurrection from the dead) are merely legends—distortions of the true historical accounts. In the view of these critics, the true Jesus of history was a great teacher; still, He was merely a man.[3] Therefore, if it can be shown that early church leaders, who personally knew the apostles or their colleagues, taught that the miraculous aspects of Christ's life actually occurred and that Jesus did in fact make the bold claims recorded in the New Testament, then this legend hypothesis fails.

A legend is a ficticious story that, through the passage of time, many people come to accept as historically accurate. A legend is able to wipe out core historical data only if the eyewitnesses and those who knew the eyewitnesses are already dead. Otherwise, the eyewitnesses or those who knew them would refute the legend. Therefore, a legend usually begins to replace accurate historical data a generation or two after the event or person in question has passed. If a written record compiled by eyewitnesses is passed on to future generations, legends can be easily refuted. If those who knew the apotles or their colleagues passed on to us accounts of Jesus, their accounts would hold great evidential weight. And, if these accounts were in general agreement with the New Testament accounts, then our confidence in the reliability of the New Testament portrait of Jesus should increase greatly.

Habermas examines the work of several apostolic fathers and their contemporaries: Clement of Rome (95AD), Ignatius (110-115AD), Polycarp (110AD), Papias (110AD), Quadratus (125AD), Barnabas (135AD), and Justin Maryr (150AD). Habermas notes that these early sources give us vital information concerning the life, teachings, death, and resurrection of Jesus.[4] Just a sample of the facts that Habermas gleaned from their writings include: 1) Jesus really did live, 2) He was born of a virgin in the city of Bethlehem, 3) He was from the tribe of Judah, 4) He was a descendant of David, 5) He was visited by Magi, 6) He was baptized by John, 7) He performed miracles and fuflilled Old Testament prophecies, 8) He preached the good news concerning the Kingdom of God, 9) He was crucified by order of Pontius Pilate, 10) He was temporarily forsaken by His friends, 11) He bodily rose from the dead, and 12) after His death, He appeared alive to His disciples on numerous occassions.[5] Several of these early church leaders also attributed deity to Jesus,[6] and wrote of the saving value of His sacrifical death.[7]

The testimony of the early second century church should be considered extremely important. Many of these early Christians were martyred for their beliefs. Since people will only die for what they truly believe, it is reasonable to conclude that the early church sincerely believed they were protecting the true apostolic faith from possible perversions. If they had tampered with the teachings of the apostles, they certainly would not have died for their counterfeit views. The apostolic fathers and early church leaders taught essentially the same things about Jesus as that taught in the New Testament, thus confirming the portrait of Jesus found on the pages of the New Testament.

ANCIENT SECULAR WRITINGS
Besides references to Christ in Christian literature which dates back to the first and second centuries AD, Habermas also refers to ancient secular writings which refer to Christ from that same time period. The significance of these non-Christian writings is that, though the secular authors themselves did not believe the early church's message, they stated the content of what the early church actually taught.

In 52AD, Thallus recorded a history of the Eastern Mediterranean world. In this work, he covered the time period from the Trojan War (mid 1200's BC) to his day (52AD). Though no manuscripts of Thallus' work are known to currently exist, Julius Africanus (writing in 221AD) referred to Thallus' work. Africanus stated that Thallus attempted to explain away the darkness that covered the land when Christ was crucified. Thallus attributed this darkness to an eclipse of the sun.[8] This reveals that about twenty years after the death of Christ, non-believers were still trying to give explanations for the miraculous events of Christ's life.

In 115AD, a Roman historian named Cornelius Tacitus wrote about the great fire of Rome which occurred during Nero's reign. Tacitus reported that Nero blamed the fire on a group of people called Christians, and he tortured them for it. Tacitus stated that the Christians had been named after their founder "Christus." Tacitus said that Christus had been executed by Pontius Pilate during the reign of Tiberius (14-37AD). Tacitus related that the "superstition" of the Christians had been stopped for a short time, but then once again broke out, spreading from Judaea all the way to Rome. He said that multitudes of Christians (based on their own confessions to be followers of Christ) were thrown to wild dogs, crucified, or burned to death. Tacitus added that their persecutions were not really for the good of the public; their deaths merely satisfied the cruelty of Nero himself.[9]

These statements by Tacitus are consistent with the New Testament records. Even Tacitus' report of the stopping of the "superstition" and then its breaking out again appears to be his attempt to explain how the death of Christ stifled the spreading of the gospel, but then the Christian message was once again preached, this time spreading more rapidly. This is perfectly consistent with the New Testament record. The New Testament reports that Christ's disciples went into hiding during His arrest and death. After Jesus rose from the dead (three days after the crucifixion), He filled His disciples with the Holy Spirit (about fifty days after the crucifixion), and they fearlessly proclaimed the gospel throughout the Roman Empire (Acts 1 and 2).

Suetonius was the chief secretary of Emperor Hadrian who reigned over Rome from 117 to 138AD. Suetonius refers to the riots that occurred in the Jewish community in Rome in 49AD due to the instigation of "Chrestus." Chrestus is apparently a variant spelling of Christ. Suetonius refers to these Jews being expelled from the city.[10] Seutonius also reports that following the great fire of Rome, Christians were punished. He refers to their religious beliefs as "new and mischievous."[11]

Pliny the Younger, another ancient secular writer, provides evidence for early Christianity. He was a Roman govenor in Asia Minor. His work dates back to 112AD. He states that Christians assembled on a set day, sangs hymns to Christ as to a god, vowed not to partake in wicked deeds, and shared "ordinary" food.[12] This shows that by 112AD, it was already common knowledge that Christians worshiped Christ, sang hymns to Him, lived moral lives, assembled regularly, and partook of common food (probably a reference to the celebration of the Lord's Supper).

The Roman Emperor Trajan also wrote in 112AD. He gave guidelines for the persecution of Christians. He stated that if a person denies he is a Christian and proves it by worshiping the Roman gods, he must be pardoned for his repentance.[13]

The Roman Emperor Hadrian reigned from 117 to 138AD. He wrote that Christians should only be punished if there was clear evidence against them. Mere accusations were not enough to condemn a supposed Christian.[14] The significance of these passages found in the writings of Trajan and Hadrian is that it confirms the fact that early Christians were sincere enough about their beliefs to die for them.

The Talmud is the written form of the oral traditions of the ancient Jewish Rabbis. A Talmud passage dating back to between 70 and 200AD refers to Jesus as one who "practised sorcery" and led Israel astray. This passage states that Jesus (spelled Yeshu) was hanged (the common Jewish term for crucifixion) on the night before the Passover feast.[15] This is a very significant passage, for it reveals that even the enemies of Christ admitted there were supernatural aspects of Christ's life by desribing Him as one who "practiced sorcery." This source also confirms that Jesus was crucified around the time of the Passover feast.

Another anti-Christian document was the Toledoth Jesu, which dates back to the fifth century AD, but reflects a much earlier Jewish tradition. In this document, the Jewish leaders are said to have paraded the rotting corpse of Christ through the streets of Jerusalem.[16] This obviously did not occur. The earliest preaching of the gospel took place in Jerusalem. Therefore, parading the rotting corpse of Christ through the streets of Jerusalem would have crushed the Christian faith in its embryonic stage. However, some of the other non-Christian authors mentioned above stated that Christianity spread rapidly during the first few decades after Christ's death. The preaching of Christ's resurrection would not have been persuasive if His rotting corpse had been publicly displayed.

It is also interesting to note that the Jewish religious leaders waited quite a long time before putting a refutation of the resurrection into print. Certainly, it would have served their best interests to disprove Christ's resurrection. But as far as written documents are concerned, the first century Jewish authorities were silent regarding the resurrection of Jesus.

Lucian was a Greek satirist of the second century. He wrote that Christians worshiped a wise man who had been crucified, lived by His laws, and believed themselves to be immortal.[17] Thus, this ancient secular source confirms the New Testament message by reporting the fact that Jesus was worshiped by His earliest followers.

Probably the most interesting of all ancient non-Christian references to the life of Christ is found in the writings of the Jewish historian named Josephus. Josephus was born in 37 or 38AD and died in 97AD. At nineteen, he became a Pharisee (a Jewish religious leader and teacher).[18] The following passage is found in his writings:

Now there was about this time Jesus, a wise man, if it be lawful to call him a man; for he was a doer of wonderful works, a teacher of such men as receive the truth with pleasure. He drew over to him both many of the Jews and many of the Gentiles. He was (the) Christ. And when Pilate, at the suggestion of the principal men amongst us, had condemned him to the cross, those that loved him at the first did not forsake him; for he appeared to them alive again the third day; as the divine prophets had foretold these and ten thousand other wonderful things concerning him. And the tribe of Christians, so named after him, are not extinct at this day.[19]

Since Josephus was a Jew and not a Christian, many scholars deny that this passage was originally written by him. These scholars believe this text was corrupted by Christians. Gary Habermas dealt with this problem in the following manner:

There are good indications that the majority of the text is genuine. There is no textual evidence against it, and, conversely, there is very good manuscript evidence for this statement about Jesus, thus making it difficult to ignore. Additionally, leading scholars on the works of Josephus have testified that this portion is written in the style of this Jewish historian. Thus we conclude that there are good reasons for accepting this version of Josephus' statement about Jesus, with modifications of questionable words. In fact, it is possible that these modifications can even be accurately ascertained. In 1972 Professor Schlomo Pines of the Hebrew University in Jerusalem released the results of a study on an Arabic manuscript containing Josephus' statement about Jesus. It includes a different and briefer rendering of the entire passage, including changes in the key words listed above. . .[20]

Habermas goes on to relate the Arabic version of this debated passage. In this version, Jesus is described as being a wise and virtuous man who had many followers from different nations. He was crucified under Pontius Pilate, but His disciples reported that, three days later, He appeared to them alive. Josephus added that Jesus may have been the Messiah whom the prophets had predicted would come.[21]

It is highly unlikely that both readings of this controversial passage are corrupt. One of these two readings probably represents the original text. The other reading would then be a copy that was tampered with by either a Christian or a non-Christian. Whatever the case may be, even the skeptic should have no problem accepting the Arabic reading. Still, even if only this reading is accepted, it is enough. For it is a first century testimony from a non-Christian historian that declares that those who knew Jesus personally claimed that He had appeared to them alive three days after His death by crucifixion under Pilate.

Several things can be learned from this brief survey of ancient non-Christian writings concerning the life of Christ. First, His earliest followers worshiped Him as God. The doctrine of Christ's deity is therefore not a legend or myth developed many years after Christ's death (as was the case with Buddha). Second, they claimed to have seen Him alive three days after His death. Third, Christ's earliest followers faced persecution and martyrdom for their refusal to deny His deity and resurrection. Therefore, the deity and resurrection of Christ were not legends added to the text centuries after its original composition. Instead, these teachings were the focus of the teaching of Christ's earliest followers. They claimed to be eyewitnesses of Christ's miraculous life and were willing to die horrible deaths for their testimonies. Therefore, they were reliable witnesses of who the true Jesus of history was and what He taught.

EVIDENCE JESUS CLAIMED TO BE GOD

Habermas builds a strong historical case that Jesus did actually consider Himself to be God incarnate. He notes that many New Testament scholars acknowledge the "Son of Man" sayings as authentic sayings of Jesus. This is because of the critical principle called "discontinuity." This principle says that a saying attributed to Jesus in the Gospels was probably actually uttered by Jesus if it was disimilar to what first-century AD Jews taught, and disimilar to what the early church taught. The reasoning of critical scholars is that if the early church taught something, then they would place those words on Jesus' lips to give authority to their beliefs. But, this cannot apply to the "Son of Man" sayings. For, though the phrase comes from Daniel chapter seven, it was not in common use by the Jews of the first century AD. Also, the church almost never used the title of Jesus, not even in New Testament times. Yet, it was the most common title Jesus used of Himself. Hence, the principle of discontinuity shows that the "Son of Man" sayings were probably uttered by Jesus Himself.[22]

But, when we look at the Son of Man sayings, we see several things that Jesus taught about Himself. Jesus predicted His death and resurrection numerous times (Mark 8:31; 9:31; 10:32-34). He claimed to be equal to God and have the power to forgive sins (Mark 2:5-12). Also, He claimed to be the Son of God and the Jewish Messiah, and He said that He would return to judge the world (Mark 14:61-64). He also claimed He came to earth to die "to give His life a ransom for many" (Mark 10:45).

Habermas also notes that when Jesus called God "Abba," He claimed to have a closeness or intimacy with the Father that no one else had.[23] When He claimed that God was His "Abba" (something as intimate as "daddy," yet more respectful), the Jews understood Jesus to be claiming to be "the Son of God" and equal to God (John 5:17-18). Some modern critics reject the passages where Jesus called Himself the Son of God. But, it is hard for New Testament critics to deny the authenticity of Mark 13:32. For, in this passage, Jesus, while calling Himself "the Son," admits that, in His human nature, He did not know the day or the hour of His return. This is an excellent example of the principle of embarrassment. The Apostles would never place these words on the lips of Jesus if He did not actually say them, for they imply a limitation of Jesus' knowledge. Hence, Jesus did make this statement, and He did think of Himself as the Son of God.

EVIDENCE JESUS ROSE FROM THE DEAD

Gary Habermas has researched the issue of Jesus' resurrection probably more than any other contemporary scholar. He has read everything in print, in English, German, and French, from the world's leading New Testament scholars, written from 1975 to nearly the present day. Habermas was able to chart their views concerning the resurrection.[24]

However, before discussing the historical data found in the New Testament that is nearly universally accepted by current New Testament critical scholarship, Habermas understands that he must answer the Scottish philosopher David Hume's objection to miracles. Hume argued that no wise man would accept the historicity of a miracle claim because the probability of a natural event will always be higher than the probability of a supernatural event. Hume believed that common experience of uninterrupted natural laws will always outweigh any supposed evidence for a miracle claim.[25]

Habermas responds by making several points. First, Hume is arguing in a cricle—he is assuming what he is supposed to prove. Hume is assuming (without argument) that common human experience is against miracles. But, there is no way to know this unless Hume already knows that no human has ever actually experienced a miracle. Second, Hume has an outdated Newtonian misunderstanding of the laws of nature—he acts as if the laws of nature prescribe what can or cannot occur. Actually, most contemporary scientists and philsoophers now understand the laws of nature to be descriptive, not prescriptive. The laws of nature describe the way nature generally operates; they do not prescribe what can or cannot occur. Third, if a theistic God exists, then miracles are possible. In other words, if a personal God exists and He is the author of the laws of nature (the way nature generally operates), then He can interrupt or supersede these laws whenever He chooses to do so. In short, Hume's a priori bias against miracles is unjustified.[26] One should not rule out miracles without examining the supposed evidence for the specific miracle claim. Having responded to Hume's objection, Habermas now turns to the historical evidence for Jesus' bodily resurrection.

His work shows that the vast majority of New Testament scholars (i.e., over 97%) acknowledge, based on the New Testament evidence, that 1) Jesus died by crucifixion, 2) his apostles' lives were transformed by what they believed were appearances to them of the resurrected Jesus, 3) Paul's life was transformed by what he believed was a post-resurrection appearance of Jesus, and 4) James' life was somehow transformed from being a mocker of His brother to being one of the key leaders in the early church. Habermas also shows that over 70% of the world's leading New Testament scholars acknowledge that the tomb was found empty early Sunday morning after Christ's crucifixion.[27] Habermas believes that the best explanation of the accepted data is that Jesus did in fact rise from the dead and appear to His disciples.

The strength of Habermas' argument for Jesus' resurrection is in the fact that he uses what the world's leading critical New Testament scholars accept to build his case for the historicity of Jesus' bodily resurrection. Most of these critics start their research with a strong bias against the resurrection. Using highly critical principles (i.e., mutiple attestation, embarrassment, discontinuity, enemy attestation, etc.), these scholars have uncovered solid historical data that they feel compelled to accept. That is the data that Gary Habermas uses to prove Jesus' resurrection.

In the case of the empty tomb, further argumention is needed. This is because only just over 70% of New Testament scholars accept the empty tomb, rather than the near universal support for the other four pieces of data. There are several reasons which show that the accounts of the empty tomb are probably historical. First, the first eyewitnesses of the empty tomb (and the resurrected Christ) were women. This is something the apostles would not have made up, for a woman's testimony was held highly suspect in the first-cenutry ad. It offered practically no evidential value to fabricate a story of women being the first witnesses.[28] Plus, the principle of embarassment applies here. For, it would have been very embarassing for the two leading apostles, Peter and John, to have been proven wrong by ladies. This would be horrible public relations for the early church. The only reason for reporting that women were the first witnesses of the empty tomb would be if it was actually true.

Second, if Jesus did not rise from the dead, then the Jewish religious authorities would have produced the rotting corpse of Christ, thus refuting Christianity and stifling its growth at its earliest stage. But this did not happen—Christianity grew at a tremendous rate in the early 30's ad in the Jerusalem area. This would not be the case if Jesus' body was still in the tomb.

Third, New Testament scholars agree that the sermons of Acts chapter 1 through 12 are the earliest sermons of the church—they date back to the early 30's ad. Their antiquity is accepted by scholars because these sermons show no signs of theological development (this type of theological development is found in Paul's letters which were written twenty years later).[29] These sermons seem to report the events of the resurrection at the earliest stage of the church. One of the main themes of these early sermons was the resurrection of Jesus. Hence, the resurrection of Jesus was reported shortly after Christ's crucifixion by people who claimed to be eyewitnesses and who were willing to suffer and die for their proclamation. Men do not die for what they know to be a hoax—they sincerely believed they saw the risen Christ.[30]

Fourth, Jesus was buried in the tomb of a well-known man—Joseph of Arimathea. It would have been easy to locate the tomb to ascertain if it was empty. Many critics acknowledge the reliability of the account of Jesus being buried in Joseph's tomb.[31] For, if there was no real Jospeh of Arimathea on the Jewish Ruling Council, then this account would be easily refuted by the enemies of the early church. However, once we admit that there existed a man named Jospeh of Arimathea on the Jewish Ruling Council, then it is highly unlikely the apostles fabricated this account. Joseph would have been easy to find—there were only 70 members on the Sanhedrin and they met regularly in Jerusalem. If the apostles lied about the burial, then one could interview Joseph of Arimathea to check the account to disprove it. But, once we admit Jesus was buried in the tomb of a famous man, then we must acknowledge how easy it would have been to prove the corpse was still in the tomb, had it actually been there. But, this did not happen. Hence, the tomb was empty.

Habermas believes the ancient creed found in 1 Corinthians 15:3-8 also provides strong evidence of the post-resurrection appearances of Jesus to His followers. In the Apostle Paul's First Letter to the Corinthians, we find excellent eyewitness testimony concerning the resurrection that nearly dates back to the event itself. The Apostle Paul wrote:

For I delivered to you as of first importance what I also received, that Christ died for our sins according to the Scriptures, and that He was buried, and that He was raised on the third day according to the Scriptures, and that He appeared to Cephas, then to the twelve. After that He appeared to more than five hundred brethren at one time, most of whom remain until now, but some have fallen asleep; then He appeared to James, then to all the apostles; and last of all, as it were to one untimely born, He appeared to me also (1 Corinthians 15:3-8).

Most New Testament scholars, liberal and conservative alike, agree that this passage is an ancient creed or hymn formulated by the early church.[32] In our task of ascertaining when the creed of 1 Corinthians 15 was created, it is first necessary to determine when Paul wrote 1 Corinthians. In this way, we will establish the latest possible date for the creed. We can then work our way back in time from that date, following any clues based upon the internal evidence found in the creed itself.

Christian philosopher J. P. Moreland, one of Habermas' colleagues, has correctly stated that for the past one hundred years almost all New Testament critics have accepted the Pauline authorship of 1 Corinthians.[33] A comparison of 1 Corinthians 16 with Acts 18, 19, and 20 provides strong evidence that 1 Corinthians was written by Paul in 55AD while in Ephesus. Scholars such as John A. T. Robinson, Henry C. Thiessen, A. T. Robertson, Douglas Moo, Leon Morris, and D. A. Carson all concur that 1 Corinthians was written in the mid 50's AD.[34]

If 55AD is the approximate date for the composition of 1 Corinthians, then the ancient creed quoted by Paul in 1 Corinthians 15:3-8 had to originate before this date. However, there is strong evidence found in the creed itself that points to its development at a much earlier time.

Habermas discusses at least eight pieces of evidence from within the creed that indicate a very early date.[35] First, the terms "delivered" and "received" have been shown to be technical rabbinic terms used for the passing on of sacred tradition. Second, Paul admitted that this statement was not his own creation and that he had received it from others. Third, scholars agree that some of the words in the creed are non-Pauline terms and are clearly Jewish. These phrases include "for our sins," "according to the Scriptures," "He has been raised," "the third day," "He was seen," and "the twelve." Fourth, the creed is organized into a stylized and parallel form; it appears to have been an oral creed or hymn in the early church. Fifth, the creed shows evidence of being of a Semitic origin and, thus, points to a source that predates Paul's translation of it into Greek. This can be seen in the use of "Cephas" for Peter, for "Cephas" is Aramaic for Peter (which is Petros in the Greek). Moreland notes additional evidence for the Semitic origin of this creed by relating that the poetic style of the creed is clearly Hebraic.[36] Sixth, Habermas reasons that Paul probably received this creed around 36-38AD, just three years after his conversion, when he met with Peter and James in Jerusalem (as recorded by Paul in Galatians 1:18-19). Jesus' death occurred around 30AD, and Paul was converted between 33 and 35AD. Seventh, Habermas states that, due to the above information, "numerous critical theologians" date the creed "from three to eight years after Jesus' crucifixion."[37] Eighth, since it would have taken a period of time for the beliefs to become formalized into a creed or hymn, the beliefs behind the creed must date back to the event itself.

As mentioned above, the antiquity of this creed is almost universally accepted across the theological spectrum of New Testament scholarship. A brief list of some of the world's leading New Testament scholars, past and present, who date the origin of this creed to the early 30's AD (just a few years after the crucifixion) will suffice: Gerd Luedemann, Marcus Borg, Reginald Fuller, Oscar Cullman, Wolfhart Panneberg, Martin Hengel, Hans Conzelman, C. H. Dodd, A. M. Hunter, James Dunn, N. T. Wright, Richard Bauckham, Rudolph Bultmann, Raymond E. Brown, Larry Hurtado, Joachim Jeremias, Norman Perrin, George E. Ladd, and Willi Marxsen.[38] Again, this list of New Testament scholars covers the theological spectrum. Some are evangelical, or at least fairly conservative in their theology and view of the Bible, while others are rather liberal in their theological and biblical perspective. Virtually, all the world's leading New Testament scholars, despite their theological perspectives, date this creed to the early 30's AD.

Habermas has provided strong evidence that the creed of 1 Corinthians 15:3-8 originated between three to eight years after Christ's crucifixion, and that the beliefs which underlie this creed must therefore go back to the event itself. Next, Habermas examines the content of this ancient creed.

First, the creed, as stated in this passage, mentions the death and burial of Christ. Second, it states that Christ was raised on the third day. Third, it lists several post-resurrection appearances of Christ. These include appearances to Peter, to the twelve apostles, to over 500 persons at one time, to James (the Lord's brother), to all the apostles, and, finally an appearance to Paul himself.

It should be noted that scholars differ as to the exact contents of this ancient creed in its most primitive form. Habermas believes that Paul added verse eight (detailing his own eyewitness account) to the original creed, as well as a portion of verse six (a reminder that most of the 500 witnesses were still alive). This in no way lessons the force of this ancient creed. In fact, it strengthens it as evidence for the resurrection, for Paul adds his own testimony and encourages his readers to question the many eyewitnesses still living in his day. Even scholars who disagree with this view still accept a large enough portion of the creed for it to be considered a valuable piece of eyewitness evidence for the resurrection of Christ from the dead.

The early date of the 1 Corinthians 15 creed proves that the resurrection accounts found in the New Testament are not legends. Christian philosopher William Lane Craig, another colleague of Gary Habermas, appealed to the work of the great Roman historian A. N. Sherwin-White and stated that "even two generations is too short a time span to allow legendary tendencies to wipe out the hard core of historical facts."[39] If two generations is not enough time for legends to develop, then there is no way that a resurrection legend could emerge in only three to eight years.

It should also be noted that, in this creed, Paul is placing his apostolic credentials on the line by encouraging his Corinthian critics to check out his account with the eyewitnesses who were still alive. These eyewitnesses not only included over 500 people, but also Peter, James, and the other apostles—the recognized leaders of the early church (Galatians 2:9). It is highly improbable that Paul would fabricate the creed and jeopardize his own position in the early church.

Finally, it should be obvious to any open-minded person who examines the evidence that Paul was a man of integrity. He was not lying. Not only did he put his reputation and position in the early church on the line, but he was also willing to suffer and die for Christ. Men do not die for what they know to be a hoax. Paul was a reliable and sincere witness to the resurrection of Christ.

Hence, the creed of 1 Corinthians 15:3-8 provides us with reliable eyewitness testimony for the bodily resurrection of Jesus Christ. Not only did Paul testify that he had seen the risen Christ, but he also identified many other witnesses to the resurrection that could have been interrogated. Contrary to the futile speculations of radical scholars, Paul was not devising myths behind closed doors. No, from the beginning he was preaching a risen Savior who had conquered death and the grave, a risen Savior who had met him on the road to Damascus and changed his life forever.

Habermas notes that the ancient creed of 1 Corinthians 15:3-8 is an example of the type of evidence that has convinced virtually all the world's leading New Testament scholars that the lives of the apostles, Paul, and James (the brother of Jesus) were radically transformed by what they believed were post-resurrection appearances of Jesus. Scholars agree that the apostles were transformed from cowardly men who fled and hid on the night Jesus was executed to courageous men willing to suffer and die for Christ. They proclaimed Jesus as the Jewish Messiah; yet, Jesus died before Israel was delivered from her pagan enemies—the Romans. When a self-proclaimed Messiah dies, his movement dies with him. When Jesus died, His Messiah movement died as well. Yet, fifty days later, at the Feast of Pentecost, it came back to life. Since a dead Messiah cannot rescue Israel from her enemies, the Messiah must have come back to life as well. The resurrection strengthened the faith of the apostles to the point that they were willing to suffer and die for Jesus.

New Testament scholars agree that Paul was a leading

persecutor of the early church. However, within a few years of the crucifixion, he was radically changed. The persecutor of the church became its greatest missionary and theologian, and one of its greatest leaders. Only Jesus' post-resurrection appearance to Paul on the Road to Damascus (Acts 9) adequately explains this radical transformation, a transformation that led to much suffering and, eventually, martyrdom.

James was an orthodox Jew and one of Jesus' brothers. During Jesus' public ministry, James was not a believer. In fact, he mocked his brother and may have even questioned his brother's sanity (John 7:3-5; Mark 3:31-35; 6:3; Matthew 13:55). This is embarassing material—the Gospels would not report this rejection of Jesus by His brothers unless it were true. Yet, in less than fifty days after the crucifixion, James became one of the most respected leaders in Jesus' church (Acts 1:14; Galatians 1:18-19; 2:9). What brought about such a drastic and abrupt change? Only Jesus' resurrection and appearance to James adequately explains how the mocking brother became a bold and courageous follower of his brother. In 62 AD, James was stoned to death for preaching his brother Jesus was the Jewish Messiah.

We must also remember that when we speak of Jesus' resurrection, we are talking about a bodily resurrection. Many people misunderstand Paul's phrase "spiritual body" in 1 Corinthians 15. They mistake this phrase for signifying some type of immaterial spirit. However, this is not the case. In the Greek, the phrase is "soma pneumatikon." The word soma almost always refers to a physical body. Still, in this passage this physical body is somehow described as being "spiritual" (pneumatikon). But, the spiritual body is contrasted with the natural body. The natural body refers to the physical body before physical death. The Greek words for natural body are "soma psuchikon." Literally, this phrase means a "soulish body." The word soul usually carries with it the idea of immateriality, but, in this passage, it cannot. It is referring to the human body before death, and, the human body is of course physical, despite the adjective "soulish." Therefore, if the "soulish body" is physical, then there should be no difficulty viewing the "spiritual body" as also being physical. The soulish body is sown (buried) at death, but, this same body is raised as a spiritual body; it receives new powers. It is no longer a natural body; it is a supernatural body. The body is changed, but it is still the same body. For, the body that was sown (buried) is the same body that will be raised. Gary Habermas discussed Christ's spiritual body in the following words:

> . . . the Gospels and Paul agree on an important fact: the resurrected Jesus had a new spiritual body. The Gospels never present Jesus walking out of the tomb. . . when the stone is rolled away, Jesus does not walk out the way He does in apocryphal literature. He's already gone, so He presumably exited through the rock. Later He appears in buildings and then disappears at will. The Gospels clearly say that Jesus was raised in a spiritual body. It was His real body, but it was changed, including new, spiritual qualities.[40]

Paul is using the term spiritual body to contrast it with the natural body. He is making the point that Christ's body after the resurrection (and ours too) has different characteristics to it than it did before. . . But the point is made very clearly that what is being talked about is the same body, the contrast here is not between physical body and spiritual body, but rather between the same body in different states or with different characteristics.[41]

Walter Martin, the foremost authority on non-Christian cults during his lifetime, also discussed Christ's spiritual body in his greatest work, Kingdom of the Cults:

> However, Christ had a "spiritual body" (1 Corinthians 15:50, 53) in His glorified state, identical in form to His earthly body, but immortal, and thus capable of entering the dimension of earth or heaven with no violation to the laws of either one.[42]

Therefore, Christ rose in the same body in which He lived and died. However, His body had been changed in the "twinkling of an eye" (1 Corinthians 15:50-53) so that His mortal body (a body capable of death) was glorified and became immortal (incapable of death). In His spiritual body, He can apparently travel at the speed of thought, unhindered by distance. The Bible teaches that in the first resurrection all believers will receive glorified bodies. Believers' bodies will be changed into glorified and immortal bodies. The presence of sin will be totally removed from them (1 Corinthians 15:50-53).

There are several good arguments that Jesus' resurrection was bodily—it was not merely a spiritual resurrection. First, as the British New Testament scholar N. T, Wright points out, the Greek words for resurrection (anistemi, anastasis, eigero, etc.), in the first century ad, always meant a reanimation of a corpse, the raising back to life of a dead body. Even those who denied the reality of resurrection always used these words to refer to bodily resurrection when denying the reality of resurrection.[43]

Second, Paul was a Pharisee (Philippiand 3:5). The Pharisees believed in the concept of physical resurrection—they believed that the children of God would be bodily raised from the dead on the last day. A non-bodily resurrection is an oxymoron.

Third, Paul believed in life after death, and that life after death started immediately following death for the believer (2 Corinthians 5:8; Philippians 1:23). But, resurrection is something that occurred after life after death. For instance, the creed of 1 Corinthians 15:3-8 states that Jesus died, was buried, and then was raised "on the third day" (vs. 4). So, as N. T. Wright says, resurrection is "life after life-after-death." The difference between life after death and "life after life-after-death" is that the former is non-bodily existence, while the latter is bodily existence. Hence, the first-century AD concept of resurrection was bodily.[44]

Fourth, the Old Testament concept of resurrection (Daniel 12; Ezekiel 37; Isaish 26:19), which was inherited by the early church, was clearly that of bodily resurrection. Fifth, Paul's writings reveal that when he spoke of resurrection he meant bodily resurrection (1 Thessalonians 4:13-18; Philippians 3:21). Sixth, 1 Corinthains 15:42-44, speaking about the resurrection body, says that that which is sown or buried is that which is raised—the same thing that is buried (i.e., the body) is the same thing that is raised (i.e., the body).

Seventh, if Paul denied the bodily resurrection and was trying to proclaim a spiritual resurrection, why not say "it is sown a soma (body), but it is raised a pneuma (spirit)?"

And, finally, the Gospel accounts of Jesus post-resurrection appearances, according to N. T. Wright, are not very theologically developed. These accounts are certainly much less theologically developed than Paul's discussions of Jesus' resurrection in his letters. Paul draws a lot of theological data from Jesus' resurrection—this implies he thought deeply about the theological implications of Jesus' resurrection. This is not the case in the Gospels—the resurrection and appearances are merely reported as historical incidents. Wright argues that this shows that the resurrection accounts in the Gospels predate Paul's writings. Since Paul began to write around 50 AD, the Gospel accounts of Jesus' resurrection and appearances must predate 50 AD.[45] Yet, in these early accounts, Jesus is reported to have bodily appeared to His disciples. He still had the scars in His hands, feet, and side. He encouraged the apostles to touch Him; He even ate food with them (John 20:26-29; Luke 24: 36-43). Together, these eight points make it clear that the early church proclaimed and believed that Jesus bodily rose from the dead.

THE FAILURE OF NATURALISTIC THEORIES

One final issue needs to be mentioned to seal Habermas' case for Christ's bodily resurrection: the failure of naturalistic theories. All alternative, non-supernatural explanations of the resurrection data fail to explain the almost universally accepted data we have mentioned. This is why the naturalistic theories of Jesus' resurrection are not popular today—they fail to explain the agreed-upon data.

The stolen body theory fails because the disciples were sincere enough in their belief that Jesus rose from the dead that they were willing to die for that belief. Men do not die for what they know to be a hoax; hence, the disciples did not steal the body and fabricate the resurrection accounts.[46]

But what if others stole the body without the disciples knowledge? This would explain the empty tomb, but not the experiences the apostles had in which they believe they saw the risen Christ numerous times. The stolen body theory simply does not adequately explain the historical data accepted by the vast majority of New Testament scholars.[47]

The wrong tomb theory fails. This alternative "explanation" speculates that maybe the women went to the wrong tomb and found it empty. They then told the disciples, who visited the same wrong tomb, also finding it empty. As a result, the disciples mistakenly proclaimed Jesus as risen from the dead. This alternative explanation fails due to the fact that the empty tomb alone did not convince the disciples that Jesus rose. They were persuaded that Jesus rose from the dead when they had experiences in which they believed He appeared to them alive from the dead. The wrong tomb theory does not explain the apostles' experiences of the post-resurrection Christ.[48]

The swoon theory is the idea that maybe Jesus merely passed out on the cross; He did not actually die. Maybe, He was revived in the tomb and was some how able to remove the large stone covering the mouth of the tomb. He then somehow travelled on scarred feet on rocky ground and appeared to His disciples. They mistook Him for risen and proclaimed Him as the Lord. This explanation fails for several reasons. First, the Roman soldier confirmed Jesus was dead with his spear thrust to Jesus' side. The Romans would confirm death before removing bodies from crosses. Second, due to the rigors of the Roman scourging and crucifixion, assuming Jesus was alive in the tomb, He would have almost certainly died due to His wounds while staying in a cold, damp tomb. Third, John records that when Jesus' side was pierced, blood and water flowed from His side. Modern medical science has proven that this only happens when the side of a corpse has been punctured—Jesus was already dead when His side was pierced. This was confirmed in the March, 1986 edition of the Journal of the American Medical Association. Fourth, even if we ignore all the above evidence against the swoon theory, it is hard to believe that the apostles would have seen Jesus in His dire, unhealthy state, and then proclaim Him as the risen Savior who has conquered death! No, they would have sought medical attention for a severely beaten, dying friend. For these reasons and others, virtually no scholars promote the swoon theory today.[49]

Finally, the hallucination theory also fails to adequately

explain the resurrection data. This view supposes that the apostles never saw the risen Christ; they merely hallucinated on numerous occassions, thinking they had seen Jesus alive from the dead. There are many problems with this theory. First, hallucinations occur inside a person's mind. Hence, no two people (let alone the apostles or over 500 people at one time) can share the same hallucination. Yet, Jesus appeared to groups of people on numerous occassions. Second, people who have hallucinations are easily convinced by others that they are mistaken. They are certainly not willing to suffer and die for their hallucinations. Third, the hallucination theory does not explain the empty tomb. Since there is good evidence for the empty tomb, this also counts against the hallucination theory. Once again, few scholars today entertain the hallucination theory.[50] Therefore, the most historically plausible explanation for the data in question is that Jesus of Nazareth did in fact bodily rise from the dead. Habermas' historical case for Jesus' bodliy resurrection is on solid epistemological ground.

CLASSIFYING HABERMAS' APOLOGETIC METHODOLOGY

Gary Habermas is willing to provide evidence for God's existence—he does so in the seminary classes he teaches as well as in some of his writings.[51] However, unlike the classical apologists, he does not believe that one must first present evidence for God's existence before presenting historical evidence for Christianity. In fact, Habermas believes that Jesus' resurrection is itself evidence for Jesus' theistic world view. In other words, Habermas believes Jesus' resurrection can be used as evidence for God.[52]

Hence, Habermas can not be classified as a classical apologist. Instead, he is an evidentialist; he can also be called a historical apologist. I use the terms interchangeably. His primary apologetic case for Christianity deals with historical evidences for Jesus' deity and resurrection. Habermas is not to be faulted for focusing almost exclusively on historical evidence for Jesus, for his dedication to researching the evidence for Jesus' resurrection has done a great service for the cause of the Gospel in these "post-Christian" days.

ENDNOTES

1. Cairns, 73.

2. Ibid.

3. Gary R. Habermas, Ancient Evidence for the Life of Jesus (Nashville: Thomas Nelson Publishers, 1984), 42.

4. Gary R. Habermas, The Historical Jesus: Ancient Evidence for the Life of Christ (Joplin: College Press, 1996), 229-242, 111-114.

5. Ibid., 239-241.

6. Ibid., 245.

7. Ibid., 233.

8. Habermas, Ancient Evidence, 93.

9. Ibid., 87-88.

10. Ibid., 90.

11. Ibid.

12. Ibid., 94.

13. Ibid., 96.

14. Ibid., 97.

15. Ibid., 98.

16. Ibid., 99-100.

17. Ibid., 100.

18. Ibid., 90.

19. Flavius Josephus, The Works of Josephus, William Whiston, trans. (Peabody: Hendrickson Publishers, 1987), 480.

20. Habermas, Ancient Evidence, 91.

21. Ibid., 91-92.

22. Gary Habermas, The Risen Jesus and Future Hope (Lanham, MD: Rowman and Littlefield Publishers, 2003), 100-106.

23. Ibid., 107.

24. Ibid., vii.

25. Ibid., 5.

26. Ibid., 5-8.

27. Gary R. Habermas and Michael R. Licona, The Case for the Resurrection of Jesus (Grand Rapids: Kregel Publications, 2004), 48-75. In The Risen Jesus and Future Hope, pages 9-10, Habermas actually lists twelve facts accepted as historical by virtually all the world's leading New Testament critics today. The twelves facts are as follows: 1) Jesus died by Roman crucifixion, 2) He was buried in a private tomb, 3) the disciples lost hope, 4) Jesus' tomb was found empty, 5) the disciples had experiences in which they believed they actually saw the risen Christ, 6) due to these experiences, the lives of the apostles were transformed to the point of being willing to suffer and die for Jesus, 7) the church proclaimed the resurrection from the earliest days, 8) the earliest preaching of the resurrection took place in Jerusalem, 9) the Gospel message focused on Jesus' death and resurrection, 10) Sunday became the primary day for worship, 11) Jesus' brother James was converted from skepticism to Christianity by what he believed was an appearance of Jesus to him, and 12) a leading persecutor of the early church, Saul of Tarsus (Paul), became a believer when he had an experience in which he believed he saw the risen Christ. Still, despite the near unanimous acceptance of these twelve facts, Habermas chooses to limit his case for the resurrection to the five facts listed in the text of this chapter. If Habermas' case for Jesus' resurrection based on the five core facts is successful, then it can only be strengthened by utilizing the additional seven facts.

28. Ibid., 70-73.

29. J. P. Moreland, Scaling the Secular City (Grand Rapids: Baker Book House, 1987), 155-156.

30. Habermas and Licona, 98.

31. Gary R. Habermas, The Historical Jesus, 152-157.

32. Moreland, 148.

33. Henry Thiessen, Introduction to the New Testament (Grand Rapids: William B. Eerdmans Publishing Company, 1987), 205.

34. John A. T. Robinson, Redating the New Testament (SCM Press, 1976), 54. Thiessen, 205. A. T. Robertson, Word Pictures in the New Testament, vol. 4. (Grand Rapids: Baker Book House, 1931), 16. D. A. Carson, Douglas J. Moo, and Leon Morris, An Introduction to

the New Testament (Grand Rapids: Zondervan Publishing House, 1992), 283.

35. Habermas, Historical Jesus, 153-157.

36. Moreland, 150.

37. Habermas, Historical Jesus, 154.

38. Ibid., 154-155.

39. William Lane Craig, Reasonable Faith (Wheaton: Crossway Books, 1984), 285.

40. Gary R. Habermas and Antony Flew, Did Jesus Rise From the Dead? (San Francisco: Harper and Row Publishers, 1987), 58.

41. Ibid., 95.

42. Walter Martin, Kingdom of the Cults (Minneapolis: Bethany House Publishers, 1977), 86.

43. N. T. Wright, The Resurrection of the Son of God (Minneapolis: Fortress Press, 2003), 31, 147-148.

44. Ibid., 31.

45. Antony Flew, There is a God (New York: Harper Collins Publishers, 2007), 202-209.

46. Habermas and Licona, 93-95.

47. Ibid., 95-97.

48. Ibid., 97-98.

49. Ibid., 99-103. For Habermas' statement concerning the JAMA article, see David Baggett, ed. Did the Resurrection Happen?A Conversation with Gary Habermas and Antony Flew (Downers Grove: Inter-Varsity Press, 2009), 25-26. Habermas notes that the three scholars who wrote the article on Jesus' death concluded that "Jesus died due to asphyxiation, complicated by shock and congestive heart failure." The journal article Habermas referred to is: William D. Edwards, Wesley J. Gabel, and Floyd Hosmer, "On the Physical Death of Jesus Christ," Journal of the American Medical Association 255 (March 1986), pp. 1455-1463.

50. Gary R. Habermas, The Resurrection of Jesus (Lanham: University Press of America, 1984), 26-27. See also Habermas and Licona, 105-109.

51. Terry L. Miethe and Gary R. Habermas, Why Believe? God Exists! (Joplin: College Press, 1993), 15-170.

52. Habermas, The Resurrection of Jesus, 67-75.

CHAPTER THREE.

Gordon Clark's
Dogmatic Presuppositionalism

....

ordon Haddon Clark (1902-1985) was one of the greatest
Christian thinkers of the twentieth century. He was the Chairman
of the Philosophy Department at Butler University for 28 years.[1]
He and Cornelius Van Til, although they disagreed on many points,
were the two leading proponents of the presuppositional method of
apologetics. In this chapter, Clark's apologetic methodology will be
examined, and its strengths and weaknesses will be discussed.

CLARK'S REJECTION OF TRADITIONAL APOLOGETICS

Gordon Clark rejected the idea that unaided human reason could
arrive at truths about God. Due to this fact, he rejected traditional
apologetics. Clark stated that "The cosmological argument for the
existence of God, most fully developed by Thomas Aquinas, is a
fallacy. It is not possible to begin with sensory experience and proceed
by the formal laws of logic to God's existence as a conclusion."[2] After
listing several reasons why he rejected the Thomistic arguments for
God's existence, Clark added that even if the arguments were valid,
they would only prove the existence of a lesser god, not the true God
of the Bible.[3]

Clark not only despised the use of philosophical arguments
to provide evidence for God's existence, but he also deplored the
utilization of historical evidences in defense of Christianity. Clark
reminded his readers that the facts of history do not come with
their own built-in interpretation. He stated that "Significance,
interpretation, evaluation is not given in any fact; it is an intellectual
judgment based on some non-sensory criterion."[4]

Clark declared that while the conclusions of science constantly
change, scriptural truth remains the same.[5] Therefore, believers

should not rely on observable facts to prove Christianity. Instead, Christians must presuppose the truth of God's Word and allow revelation to interpret the facts of history for them.[6]

The reason behind Clark's distaste for traditional apologetics was his belief that unaided human reason could never discover any truth, religious or secular. This, Clark believed, should convince a person of his need to presuppose the truth of the Christian revelation.[7] Without this presupposition, man cannot find truth. Clark emphasized this point at the conclusion of his textbook on the history of philosophy. He stated, "Does this mean that philosophers and cultural epochs are nothing but children who pay their fare to take another ride on the merry-go-round? Is this Nietzsche's eternal recurrence? Or, could it be that a choice must be made between skeptical futility and a word from God?"[8]

CLARK'S REJECTION OF EMPIRICISM

Empiricism is the attempt to find truth through the five senses. This school of thought believes "that all knowledge begins in sense experience."[9] According to Clark, Thomas Aquinas was an empiricist. Aquinas believed that "all knowledge must be abstracted out of our sensations."[10] Aquinas believed that each person begins life with his mind as a blank slate. He held that "everything that is in the mind was first in the senses, except the mind itself."[11] Although Aquinas believed that God created man's mind with the innate ability to know things and draw rational conclusions from sense data, Clark does not seem to do justice to this aspect of Aquinas' thought.[12] Instead, he merely attacks the idea that man could argue from sense data to the existence of God.

Clark turns next to William Paley. Paley argued from the evidence of design in the universe to the existence of an intelligent God as its Cause. Therefore, he, like Aquinas, began with sense experience and then argued to the existence of God. Clark agreed with the criticisms made by David Hume concerning the teleological argument (the argument for God's existence from design). Hume stated that experience cannot determine if there was one God or several gods who designed the world. Second, since the physical world is finite, nothing in man's experience tells him that its designer must be infinite. And third, since human experience includes such things as natural disasters, might not the world's designer be an evil being?[13]

Clark pointed out that Hume himself was an empiricist. But Hume was consistent in his thinking. Therefore, he realized that the principle of cause and effect, the existence of external bodies, and the reality of internal selves could not be proven through sense data alone. Therefore, Hume admitted that his empiricism inevitably led to skepticism.[14]

Clark emphasized the point that there is a wide gap between basic sense experience and the propositional conclusions made by empiricists.[15] Sense data (the facts of experience) do not come with their own built-in interpretation. Rational conclusions cannot come from sense experience alone. Empiricism, therefore, fails as a truth-finding method. Next, Gordon Clark turned his attention to rationalism.

CLARK'S REJECTION OF RATIONALISM

Rationalism is the attempt to find truth through reason alone. Though Clark admitted that Augustine was not a pure rationalist, he discussed his views of reason.[16] At a time when Greek philosophy was dominated by skepticism, which argued against the possibility of attaining knowledge, Augustine attempted to find a base for knowledge that could not be denied.[17] Augustine declared that "the skeptic must exist in order to doubt his own existence." Augustine therefore reasoned that even the skeptic should be certain of his existence. Augustine also showed that skeptics could not live like knowledge was impossible.[18]

Augustine also held that the laws of logic were universal, eternal, and unchanging truths. Since the human mind is limited and changing, it could not be the ultimate source of these eternal truths. Hence, there must be an eternal and unchanging Mind as their source. Obviously, this eternal Mind is God.[19]

Clark critiqued the views of Anselm. Anselm was even more rationalistic in his thought than Augustine. He believed that the existence of God could be proven through reason alone. Anselm referred to God as the greatest conceivable Being. Therefore, if

God does not exist, then one could conceive of a being greater than Him, a being that has the same attributes but does exist. But then this would be the greatest conceivable Being. Therefore, God (the greatest conceivable Being) must necessarily exist.[20] This is called the ontological argument for God's existence.

Clark wrote that Rene Descartes, also a rationalist, viewed sensation and experience as very deceptive. He attempted to find a single point of certainty by doubting everything until he found something he could not doubt. Through this process, he realized that the more he doubted, the more certain he became of the existence of himself, the doubter.[21]

Descartes borrowed Anselm's ontological argument for God's existence. Clark stated Descartes' version of this argument as follows: "God, by definition, is the being who possesses all perfections; existence is a perfection; therefore God exists."[22]

Clark related that Spinoza also used the ontological argument for God's existence. But Spinoza's version of the argument did not conclude with the God of the Bible. Instead he "proved" the existence of a god who is the universe (the god of pantheism).[23] However, this raised questions as to rationalism's claim to prove the existence of God with certainty, for Spinoza's god and Descartes' God cannot both exist. Spinoza was also more consistent in his rationalism than was Descartes. Spinoza realized that if all knowledge could be found through reason alone, then supernatural revelation is without value.[24]

Gordon Clark listed several problems with rationalism in his writings. He stated that rationalism has historically led to several contradictory conclusions (theism, pantheism, and atheism).[25] Also, Clark stated that "rationalism does not produce first principles out of something else: The first principles are innate . . . Every philosophy must have its first principles . . . Thus a presuppositionless description is impossible."[26] Although Clark made much use of reason in his own defense of the faith, he presupposed his first principles. He contended that without doing this, reason can never get off the ground.[27]

CLARK'S REJECTION OF IRRATIONALISM

In discussing the history of philosophy, Clark stated that "Hume had reduced empiricism to skepticism."[28] Immanuel Kant's views left man with a knowledge of "things-as-they-appear-to-us," but with no real knowledge of "things-in-themselves."[29] Clark emphasized this point with the following words: "In his view the uninformed sense data are entirely incoherent. Order is introduced into them by the mind alone, and what the real world might be like. . . remains unknowable. The whole Postkantian development from Jacobi to Hegel convicts Kant of skepticism."[30]

Clark added that though Hegel effectively critiqued Kant, Hegelianism also failed to justify knowledge.[31] In Hegel's theory of the unfolding of history, truth was seen as relative. What was true yesterday is not necessarily true today.[32] In short, the greatest minds the world has ever known have failed to escape skepticism. The philosophy of man cannot even prove that man can know anything. Empiricism and rationalism have both failed. This has caused some thinkers to accept irrationalism as the method of finding meaning to life. One such thinker was Soren Kierkegaard.

Kierkegaard denied the effectiveness of both reason and sense experience in finding truth. He believed that a man must stop reasoning. Only through a blind leap of faith can man find true meaning in life. An individual's subjective passion is of more importance than objective truth. Kierkegaard believed that the doctrines of Christianity were absurd and contradictory. Still, he chose to believe against all reason.[33]

Clark rejected the irrationalism of Kierkegaard even though it had become so widespread among modern thinkers, both secular and religious. Clark stated of Kierkegaard, "The fatal flaw is his rejection of logic. When once a man commits himself to contradictions, his language, and therefore his recommendations to other people, become meaningless."[34]

As shown above, Gordon Clark rejected empiricism, rationalism, and irrationalism. He taught that they all eventually reduce to skepticism. Man has failed to find truth through these methodologies. Therefore, man, according to Clark, must make a choice between skepticism and a word from God.[35] Clark's method of finding truth is called presuppositionalism or dogmatism.

CLARK'S VIEW: DOGMATISM

When one finds that Clark saw all of secular philosophy as unable to justify knowledge, one might assume that Clark was himself a skeptic. But this was not the case. Skeptical futility is not the only option left. Clark referred to his view of finding truth as dogmatism. Clark argued that if all other philosophical systems cannot give meaning to life, then dogmatism is worth a try. Clark recommended that one dogmatically presuppose the truth of the teachings of Scripture.[36]

Clark's view may seem to some to be fideism. But this is not so (according to Clark). For everyone, no matter what their philosophical system may be, must presuppose something.[37] The rationalist must presuppose his first principles. Otherwise, he must look for reasons for everything. This would result in an infinite regress, and there would be no real base for knowledge.[38]

The empiricist must assume certain concepts which he cannot prove through sense experience. Such concepts as time, space, equality, causality, and motion are not derived from sense experience. They are brought into one's sense experience in the beginning to aid one in drawing conclusions from the sense data.[39] Logical Positivism is an extreme empirical view. One of its first principles is that truth can only be found through the five senses. However, this first principle refutes itself since it cannot itself be proven through the five senses.[40]

Clark argued that since rationalism and empiricism have failed to make life meaningful, Christian presuppositions should be utilized. For Christian presuppositions do give meaning to life.[41] Clark argued that "Christian Theism is self-consistent and that several other philosophies are inconsistent, skeptical, and therefore erroneous."[42] Clark added that Christianity "gives meaning to life and morality, and that it supports the existence of truth and the possibility of knowledge."[43]

One can see Clark's point more clearly by examining his critique of Kant. In Kant's thinking, there existed no order in sense data. Instead the mind introduces this order into the sense data. Therefore, Kant's view collapses into skepticism since one can only know things-as-they-appear-to-us and not things-as-they-are. One cannot know the real world. One can only know the world as it appears to him.[44]

Clark's response to Kant's dilemma is as follows. Clark presupposes the truth of the revelation found in Scripture. Therefore, Clark presupposes that "God has fashioned both the mind and the world so that they harmonize."[45] If one presupposes the truth of Christianity, then the order that the mind innately reads into the real world is the order which really exists in the real world.

Having discussed Clark's view of obtaining knowledge, one must now consider how Clark defended Christianity. Clark did this by convincing the nonbeliever that he is contradicting himself.[46] Clark was willing to use logic (the law of noncontradiction) to refute the belief systems of others. He did not feel that he was being inconsistent with his presuppositionalism or dogmatism, for Clark believed that God is Logic. In other words, logic is God-thinking. It flows naturally from God's Being.[47] In fact, Clark even translated John 1:1 as, "In the beginning was Logic, and Logic was with God, and Logic was God."[48]

The problem with rationalism is that it lacks sufficient first principles. But, according to Clark, once one presupposes the truth of the Bible, one can use reason to tear down the views of others. Clark spoke of reason in the following manner:

> Therefore I wish to suggest that we neither abandon reason nor use it unaided; but on pain of skepticism acknowledge a verbal, propositional revelation of fixed truth from God. Only by accepting rationally comprehensible information on God's authority can we hope to have a sound philosophy and a true religion.[49]

Clark not only defended the faith by tearing down other belief systems through use of the law of contradiction, but he (after presupposing the truth of Christianity) also was willing to confirm the truth of Christianity in two ways. First, Clark showed that it alone is self-consistent. And second, he appealed to its ability to provide man with meaning to life, moral values, and the genuine possibility of attaining true knowledge.[50] Since all other philosophies have failed to obtain knowledge, one must choose between skepticism and presupposing Christian revelation.[51]

Still, Clark seemed to revert back to fideism. This was due to his hyper-Calvinistic theology. He firmly believed that one really cannot convince another of the truth of Christianity, for God alone sovereignly bestows faith upon an individual.[52] When answering the question of why one person presupposes the Bible to be true and not the Muslim Koran, he simply replied that "God causes the one to believe."[53]

CLARK'S SOLUTION TO THE PROBLEM OF EVIL

In his writings, Gordon Clark attempted to answer the question, "How can the existence of God be harmonized with the existence of evil?"[54] If God is all-good, He would want to destroy evil. If God is all-powerful, He is able to destroy evil. But evil still exists. It seems that God cannot be both all-good and all-powerful. However, Christianity teaches that He is both. This is the problem of evil.[55] Zoroastrianism attempts to resolve the problem by teaching that there are two gods. One is good while the other is evil. Neither of the two gods is infinite since they have both failed to destroy the opposing god. Plato's views also result in an unresolved dualism. In his thought, God is not the creator of all things. There exists eternal and chaotic space which the Demiurge cannot control.[56]

According to Clark, even Augustine's answer to the dilemma was inadequate. Clark stated that Augustine taught that evil is metaphysically unreal. It does not exist. Therefore, all that God created is good since evil is non-being.[57] (Whether or not Clark treated Augustine's view fairly will be discussed at a later point in this chapter.)

Clark pointed out that Augustine added to his response the doctrine of human free will. Though God is all-powerful, He has sovereignly chosen to give mankind free will. God allows man to make his own choices. Mankind has chosen evil. Therefore, all that God created is good. Evil can be blamed not on God, but on the abuse of free will by man.[58]

But Clark rejected this view of free will. Clark believed that the Bible does not teach that man is free to choose that which is right as opposed to that which is wrong. Clark stated that "free will is not only futile, but false. Certainly, if the Bible is the Word of God, free will is false; for the Bible consistently denies free will."[59]

Though Clark rejected the doctrine of free will, he believed man has free agency. "Free will means there is no determining factor operating on the will, not even God. Free will means that either of two incompatible actions are equally possible."[60] This Clark rejected. On the other hand, "Free agency goes with the view that all choices are inevitable. The liberty that the Westminster Confession ascribes to the will is a liberty from compulsion, coaction, or force of inanimate objects; it is not a liberty from the power of God."[61] Clark argued that a man can still be responsible for his actions even without the freedom to do other than he has done. Clark stated that, "a man is responsible if he must answer for what he does . . . a person is responsible if he can be justly rewarded or punished for his deeds. This implies, of course, that he must be answerable to someone."[62]

Clark then asked the question, "Is it just then for God to punish a man for deeds that God Himself 'determined before to be done?'"[63] He answered in the affirmative. He stated that, "Whatever God does is just."[64] Man is responsible to God; but God is responsible to no one.

Clark openly admitted that his view makes God the cause of sin. For, in his thinking, "God is the sole ultimate cause of everything."[65] But, while God is the ultimate cause of sin, He is not the author of sin. The author is the immediate cause of an action. Man is the immediate cause of his sin. But he was not free to do otherwise. For God is the ultimate cause of sin.[66]

Clark stated that, "God's causing a man to sin is not sin. There is no law, superior to God, which forbids him to decree sinful acts. Sin presupposes a law, for sin is lawlessness."[67] Clark explained that "God is above law" because "the laws that God imposes on men do not apply to the divine nature."[68] Clark stated:

> Man is responsible because God calls him to account; man is responsible because the supreme power can punish him for disobedience. God, on the contrary, cannot be responsible for the plain reason that there is no power superior to him; no greater being can hold him accountable; no one can punish him; there is no

one to whom God is responsible; there are no laws which he could disobey. The sinner therefore, and not God, is responsible; the sinner alone is the author of sin. Man has no free will, for salvation is purely of grace; and God is sovereign.[69]

This was Clark's proposed solution to the problem of evil. God is in fact the ultimate cause of sin. But He is not evil, for He committed no sin. And He is not responsible for sin, for there is no one to whom He is responsible. God is just, for whatever He does is just. Therefore, the creature has no right to stand in judgment over his Creator.

STRENGTHS OF CLARK'S PRESUPPOSITIONALISM

Gordon Clark, as this study shows, was a very original thinker. Even if one disagrees with much of what he has written, he has made a tremendous contribution to Christian thought that should not be overlooked. There are several strengths which are evident in the thought of Gordon Clark.

His rejection of pure rationalism. Clark is absolutely correct when he points out the major deficiency of rationalism. That is, rationalism cannot even get started until certain unproven assumptions are made. Reason cannot prove everything. This would result in an infinite regress, and nothing would be proven. First principles must be presupposed. They are not logically necessary (they cannot be proven with rational certainty).

His rejection of pure empiricism. Clark is right when he points out problems with extreme empiricism. Sense data and the facts of history do not come with their own built-in interpretations. They must be interpreted within the context of a person's world view. Empirical data alone cannot give us rational conclusions.

His rejection of irrationalism. Clark should be commended for his lack of patience for irrationalism. Once a person denies the law of contradiction, then the opposite of whatever that person teaches can be equally true with those teachings. But all human thought and communication comes to a halt if one allows such an absurd premise. A person who holds to irrationalism cannot even express his view without assuming the truth of the law of contradiction.

His knowledge of the history of philosophical thought. Rarely does one read the works of a Christian author who has the insights that Clark had. His knowledge of the thought of the great philosophical minds of the past should encourage all Christians to be more diligent in their own studies. Gordon Clark was a man who had something to say because he was a man who lived a disciplined life of study. Even if one disagrees with the thrust of Clark's thought, one must never dismiss the insights he shared with others concerning the history of philosophy.

His recognition of the fact that all people have hidden presuppositions. Too often Christians pretend that they have no biases whatsoever, but this is not the case. Every person, believer and nonbeliever alike, has presuppositions that are often hidden. Clark was right in his view that apologetics is more accurately the seeking of confirmation for our presuppositions than it is the unbiased search for truth.

His use of the law of noncontradiction. Clark was justified in his usage of the law of noncontradiction. If two opposite concepts can both be true at the same time and in the same sense, then all knowledge and communication become impossible. Any world view that either is a contradiction or generates contradictions is not worth believing.

He is very consistent in his Calvinism. Too often Christians claim to be Calvinists but actually deny or redefine several of the five main points of Calvinism. Clark is not only a strong defender of all five points, but he also consistently holds to the implications of these points. His rejection of human free will and his view of God as the ultimate cause of evil are unpopular concepts, even among Calvinists. Clark is to be credited with having the courage to believe that which is consistent with his system of thought.

He is right to seek confirmation for his Christian presuppositions. Many presuppositionalists are content in merely assuming the truth of Christianity. But Clark realizes that, after presupposing biblical truth, one must still seek justification for this assumption. Clark does this by showing that Christianity does what all secular philosophies have failed to do. They failed to give meaning to life, justify moral values, and find truth.

He is right that man must choose. Clark recognizes that since all secular philosophies have failed to justify their truth claims, man must make a choice. A person can choose to continue to live with contradictory views. Or a person can choose skepticism and suspend all judgment (except his judgment to be skeptical). Clark even remarks that, for some, suicide is their choice.[70] But Clark pleads with his readers to choose Christianity. If secular philosophies have failed to find truth and give meaning to life, then why not choose Christianity? Whatever the case, man must choose.

THE WEAKNESSES OF CLARK'S PRESUPPOSITIONALISM

His denial of the basic reliability of sense perception. Though Clark is correct when he states that concepts such as moral values, causality, time, and space cannot be derived from sense data alone, he goes too far when he speaks of the "futility of sensation."[71] With Clark's distrust for sense experience, how can he presuppose the truth of the Bible? For he must first use his sense of sight to read the Bible to find out what it is he is going to presuppose. In fact, the Bible itself seems to teach the basic reliability of sense perception. The Mosaic Law places great emphasis on eyewitness testimony, and the eyewitness accounts of Christ's post-resurrection appearances are presented as evidence for the truth of Christ's claims.

His denial of Thomistic first principles. While refuting rationalism, Clark stated that it needed first principles. For justification must stop somewhere. He pointed out that since first principles could not be proven through reason alone, rationalism fails to find truth without appealing to something other than reason. The first principles are not logically necessary. In this he is correct. However, Clark accepts the law of contradiction (what Thomists call the law of noncontradiction), though he says it is not logically necessary. He points out that if we do not accept this law, all knowledge and communication would cease. However, this is the same type of argument that Aquinas (and Aristotle long before him) used for his remaining first principles. Besides the principle of noncontradiction, Aquinas utilized the principles of identity, excluded middle, causality, and finality.[72] Aristotle and Aquinas argued that these principles "cannot actually be denied without absurdity."[73] In other words, they are actually undeniable (though not logically necessary). But this is very similar to what Clark claims for one of his first principles, the law of contradiction. If Clark is justified in using this principle, then the other Thomistic first principles of knowledge may likewise be justified. If one accepts the principle of causality (every effect has an adequate cause), then one can reason from the effect (the finite world) to its cause (the infinite Creator). This would deal Clark's entire system a lethal blow since it would justify the use of traditional arguments for God's existence. This would eliminate presuppositional apologetics as the only way for a Christian to defend his faith.

His downplaying of historical evidences for the Christian Faith. Clark rightly criticized deriving knowledge from sense data alone. Because of this, he minimized historical evidences. For facts of history, like sense data, do not come with their own built-in interpretations. However, if one accepts Thomistic first principles (because they are actually undeniable), then one can attempt to make sense of the facts of history. If a man claimed to be God and rose from the dead to prove His claim true, then one is not justified in explaining this resurrection in purely naturalistic terms. For every event must have an adequate cause. And no naturalistic explanation has succeeded to account for the resurrection.[74] Only a supernatural cause is sufficient in this case.

He gives no credit to probability arguments. Clark points out that other systems of philosophy do not have a starting point based on certainty. They must presuppose their first principles. However, Clark's own first principles are also not based on certainty; they too must be presupposed. It seems that Clark is judging his own philosophical system in a more lenient fashion than he does other schools of thought. It is true that Clark finds confirmation for the Christian presupposition that is lacking in other presuppositions. Still, this is after the fact. And, as Clark admits, this confirmation itself only makes Christianity more probable than other views; it does not establish its certainty. It seems that more credit should be given to arguments for first principles based upon a high degree of probability. Why should an argument be rejected when its premises and conclusion are very probable, while opposing views are unlikely? Other philosophers have settled for less than certainty but still have solid systems of thought. Some might argue from premises that they believe are "beyond all reasonable doubt." Norman Geisler, following in the tradition of Thomas Aquinas, uses the principle of "actual undeniability."[75] Some things cannot be denied without contradiction and therefore must be true. For instance, if I deny my existence I must first exist to make the denial. For nothing is nothing. Nothing cannot deny anything. Only an existent being can deny something. Therefore, it is actually undeniable that I exist.[76]

Charles Hodge (1797-1878) based his philosophical arguments on what he believed were "self-evident truths." Though these truths could be denied by others, their denial is "forced and temporary." Once a philosopher finishes lecturing or debating, he returns to the real world and no longer denies self-evident truths such as his existence, the existence of others, and the reality of moral values.[77] He can deny moral values in the lecture hall, but once he is at home, he calls the police when he is robbed.

It seems then that Clark is mistaken. Christians can discover truths that are either "self-evident" or "actually undeniable." They can then dialogue with nonbelievers using these premises as common ground. Clark was wrong not to give proper due to first principles based upon a high degree of probability. This leaves the door open for traditional apologetics.

His attacks on traditional apologetics. Clark's attack on traditional apologetics is unfounded. This can be shown from his treatment of the Thomistic cosmological argument for God's existence. Aquinas argued that all existent beings which could possibly not exist need a cause or ground for their continuing in existence. In other words, all dependent existence must rely for its continued existence on a totally independent Being, a Being which is uncaused and self-existent.[78]

Clark comments that Aquinas has not ruled out the possibility of an infinite regress of dependent beings.[79] However, Clark is mistaken. For Aquinas is not arguing indefinitely into the past. He is arguing for the current existence of a totally independent Being. Aquinas is arguing for the cause of the continued and present existence of dependent beings, not just the cause for the beginning of their existence.[80] Aquinas is pointing out that if one takes away the independent Being, then there is nothing to sustain the existence of all dependent beings. Every dependent being relies directly on the independent Being for preserving it in existence. The causality is simultaneous, just as a person's face simultaneously causes the existence of its reflection in a mirror. At the exact moment the person moves his face, the reflection is gone.

Clark raises another objection against the Thomistic cosmological argument. He states that even if the argument is valid, it would not prove the existence of the God of the Bible. Clark seems to imply that unless we prove every attribute of God, then it is not the identical God.[81] However, if Aquinas proves the existence of the Uncaused Cause of all else that exists, how could this possibly not be the God of the Bible? If Clark can refer to God as "Truth" and "Logic" and still be talking about the Triune God of the Bible, then Aquinas can identify God with the "Unmoved Mover."

Finally, Clark accuses Aquinas of using the word "exist" with two completely different meanings.[82] When Aquinas speaks of God, he speaks of God existing infinitely. But when he speaks of man, he speaks of man existing finitely. God is existence; man merely has existence. Though Clark's critique may seem valid, it is not. Aquinas would define existence as "that which is" whether it referred to God or man. True, Aquinas would apply the term "existence" to God infinitely, but to man only finitely. Still, the fact remains that whether Aquinas speaks of God or man, the meaning of existence remains the same.

Apparently, Clark misunderstands Aquinas' view of analogical language. Aquinas taught that we cannot have univocal (totally the same) knowledge of God. Still, our knowledge of God is not equivocal (totally different) since that would be no knowledge at all. Instead, according to Aquinas, our knowledge of God is analogical (similar). By this Aquinas did not mean that the concepts used of God and man have similar meanings. He meant that they have identical meanings, but that they must be applied only in a similar way. All limitations must be removed from a concept before it is applied to God. However, the concept itself continues to have the same meaning throughout.[83]

Not only did Clark express distaste for the cosmological argument for God's existence, he also disliked the teleological argument (the argument from design).[84] He accepted Hume's criticism of this argument. Hume concluded that it proved the existence only of a finite god or gods, and that this god or gods may be evil (due to the evil in the world). However, if one argues for the existence of one infinite God through the cosmological argument, and then finishes the argument with the teleological premises, the argument from design will add the attribute of intelligence to the Uncaused Cause. The problem of evil could also be dealt with as a separate issue. In short, Clark's attempt to destroy traditional apologetics has failed.

His failure to refute the Islamic Faith. After destroying secular philosophy through the use of the law of contradiction, Clark does not apply this law to Islam. Instead, he merely states that God causes some to accept the Bible when answering the question, "Why does one man accept the Koran and another the Bible?"[85] Apparently, after all is said and done, Clark's system relies on God alone to cause the person to believe. One wonders why Clark went to such trouble to refute secular philosophies. Could not the same response be given to them?

His misrepresentation of Augustine and Aquinas. While dealing with the problem of evil, Clark accused Augustine of denying the reality of evil. He stated that Augustine taught that "all existing things are good" and that "evil therefore does not exist—it is metaphysically unreal."[86] Clark represented Augustine as reasoning that since evil does not exist, God cannot be the cause of evil.[87] In this way, Clark makes it sound as if Augustine is in agreement with the Christian Science view of evil as an illusion. Clark is misrepresenting Augustine on this point.

Augustine did teach that God created everything that exists and that all that God created is good. However, evil is a perversion of that good brought about by the free choices of rational beings (fallen angels and men). Evil is a privation. It is a lack of a good that should be there.[88] An illustration of this would be rust. God did not create rust. Still it exists, but only as a corruption of something that

God created (metal). Therefore, evil is real, but it must exist in some good thing that God created. All that God created is good. God did not create evil. He created the possibility of evil (free will). Fallen rational beings actualized evil by abusing a good thing (free will) God gave them.

Clark also misrepresents Aquinas by downplaying Aquinas' emphasis on the active mind. It is true that Aquinas believed all knowledge comes through sense experience, but he also taught that God created man's mind with the innate ability to draw rational conclusions from sense data. Aquinas spoke of both the active mind (this innate ability to arrive at universals from particulars) and the receptive mind (the aspect of the mind which receives data from sense experience). Clark focuses on Aquinas' doctrine of the receptive mind, while de-emphasizing Aquinas' teaching about the active mind (also called the agent intellect).[89]

His proposed solution to the problem of evil. Clark's answer to the problem of evil is inadequate. He stated that God is not responsible for evil simply because there is no one above Him to whom He is responsible. Since Clark denied human free will (man could not choose to do otherwise), Clark made God the ultimate cause of evil.

The Augustinian approach, in the opinion of many Christian philosophers, is to be preferred. Augustine held that God gave man the freedom to disobey His commands. Therefore, God permitted sin; it was not part of His perfect will for man. A free will theodicy (attempting to propose a reason why God permitted evil) or a free will defense (attempting to merely show that it is not impossible for an all-good and all-powerful God to coexist with evil) is a much more plausible solution to the problem of evil than the solution Clark proposed.[90] Of course, since Clark denied genuine free will, these options were not open to him.

He does not allow for the use of secular material during evangelism. Clark states, "in evangelistic work there can be no appeal to secular, non-Christian material."[91] However, this is exactly what the apostle Paul did on Mars Hill. When speaking to Stoic and Epicurean philosophers, he quoted from the writings of two ancient Greek poets to find common ground with his hearers (Acts 17:16-34). If one must choose between the evangelistic approach of Gordon Clark and that of the apostle Paul, then one should choose Paul.

No Christian can show that every non-Christian system of thought is inconsistent. Clark claims that since every non-Christian philosophy has failed, people should presuppose the truth of the Christian world view. However, it is impossible for Clark, or any other person, to thoroughly examine every non-Christian system of thought.[92] Even if it were possible for Clark to expose the contradictions in every non-Christian world view today, there is no guarantee that a totally consistent non-Christian world view will not be produced in the future.[93]

POSTSCRIPT: TWO DISTINCT METHODOLOGIES?

Christian philosopher Ronald Nash has made an interesting observation concerning Gordon Clark's epistemology (theory of knowledge) and apologetic methodology. Nash believes that Gordon Clark's view of knowledge and his apologetic methodology had changed by the closing years of his ministry and life.[94] The early Clark was a proponet of dogmatic presuppositionalism. Clark believed that we must presuppose our first principles and then deduce all other truth from these starting points. Clark reasoned that the world view whose first principles explained the data without contradictions was the true world view. Clark dogmatically presupposed the existence of the Triune God who has revealed Himself in Scripture and the law of contradiction. According to Clark, this world view alone produced an internally consistent view of reality.

However, Nash contends that Clark's views changed later in his career. By the close of Clark's career, Clark promoted a view called Scripturalism. In this view, truth can only be deduced from the Bible and the Bible alone.[95] Only in the Bible can truth be found. Nash points out that this is a very weak view of knowledge since one cannot deduce one's own existence from the Scriptures.[96] Nash also pointed out that a person has to use their senses in order to know what the Bible says; yet, Scripturalism does not allow for any truth to be obtained through the senses. Truth can only be found in the Bible.

CONCLUSION

Assuming that Ronald Nash is correct in his assessment of Gordon Clark's shift in thought, Clark's later approach to apologetics (Scripturalism) fails. It is pure fideism—it accepts the Scriptures, and only what the Scriptures teach, by blind faith. Scripturalism fails to explain how we can even know what the Bible teaches since it rejects knowledge attained through sense perception. A scripturalist has no way to respond to a Muslim, someone who chooses to presuppose the Koran (a different "holy book").

Still, Clark's earlier presuppositional approach to apologetics (dogmatic presuppositionalism), with minor adaptions, is a worthy apologetic. Uncovering contradictions in non-Christian belief systems is a necessary component in one's defense of the faith. However, Clark's presuppositional approach is not the only method Christians can use when defending the faith. Although Clark successfully demolishes several secular philosophies, traditional apologetics survives his assault.

ENDNOTES

1. Gordon H. Clark, Clark Speaks From the Grave (Jefferson: The Trinity Foundation, 1986), 2.

2. Gordon H. Clark, Religion, Reason and Revelation (Jefferson: The Trinity Foundation, 1986), 35.

3. Ibid., 37.

4. Clark, Clark Speaks From the Grave, 54.

5. Ibid., 55.

6. Ibid., 57.

7. Geisler, Christian Apologetics, 37.

8. Gordon H. Clark, Thales to Dewey (Jefferson: The Trinity Foundation, 1989), 534.

9. Norman L. Geisler and Paul D. Feinberg, Introduction to Philosophy: A Christian Perspective (Grand Rapids: Baker Book House, 1985), 431.

10. Gordon H. Clark, Three Types of Religious Philosophy (Jefferson: The Trinity Foundation, 1989), 60-61.

11. Geisler, Thomas Aquinas, 86.

12. Ibid.

13. Clark, Three Types of Religious Philosophy, 64-70.

14. Ibid., 71,76-78.

15. Ibid., 91.

16. Ibid., 27.

17. Ibid., 28-29.

18. Ibid., 31.

19. Ibid., 32.

20. Ibid., 33-35.

21. Clark, Religion, Reason and Revelation, 50-51.

22. Clark, Three Types of Religious Philosophy, 35.

23. Clark, Thales to Dewey, 332.

24. Clark, Religion, Reason and Revelation, 53.

25. Clark, Three Types of Religious Philosophy, 56.

26. Ibid., 117-118.

27. Ibid., 120.

28. Ibid., 93.

29. Clark, Religion, Reason and Revelation, 62.

30. Gordon H. Clark, A Christian View of Men and Things (Jefferson: The Trinity Foundation, 1991), 315-316.

31. Clark, Religion, Reason and Revelation, 63-68.

32. Ibid., 98.

33. Clark, Three Types of Religious Philosophy, 101-105.

34. Ibid., 114.

35. Clark, Thales to Dewey, 534.

36. Clark, Three Types of Religious Philosophy, 116.

37. Ibid., 118.

38. Ibid., 51-52.

39. Ibid., 70-91.

40. Ibid., 118-119.

41. Clark, A Christian View of Men and Things, 324.

42. Ibid.

43. Ibid.

44. Ibid., 315-316.

45. Ibid., 316.

46. Clark, Three Types of Religious Philosophy, 140-142.

47. R. C. Sproul, John Gerstner, and Arthur Lindsley, Classical Apologetics: A Rational Defense of the Christian Faith and a Critique of Presuppositional Apologetics (Grand Rapids: Zondervan Books, 1984), 76.

48. Ibid.

49. Clark, Religion, Reason and Revelation, 87.

50. Clark, A Christian View of Men and Things, 324.

51. Clark, Religion, Reason and Revelation, 109-110.

52. Clark, Three Types of Religious Philosophy, 138.

53. Ibid., 139.

54. Clark, Religion, Reason and Revelation, 195.

55. Ibid.

56. Ibid., 195-196.

57. Ibid., 196.

58. Ibid., 199.

59. Ibid., 206.

60. Ibid., 227.

61. Ibid.

62. Ibid., 231.

63. Ibid.

64. Ibid., 232-233.

65. Ibid., 237-238.

66. Ibid., 237-239.

67. Ibid., 239-240.

68. Ibid., 240.

69. Ibid., 241.

70. Clark, Thales to Dewey, 534.

71. Clark, Three Types of Religious Philosophy, 91.

72. Geisler, Thomas Aquinas, 72-74.

73. Ibid., 78-79.

74. Habermas, 26-33.

75. Geisler, Christian Apologetics, 143.

76. Ibid., 143-144.

77. Charles Hodge, Systematic Theology (Grand Rapids: Eerdmans Publishing Company, 1989), vol. 1, 210.

78. Thomas Aquinas, Summa Theologiae, 1a. 2,3.

79. Clark, Religion, Reason and Revelation, 36-37.

80. Craig, Apologetics, 63-65.

81. Clark, Religion, Reason and Revelation, 37-38.

82. Ibid., 38-39.

83. Geisler, Thomas Aquinas, 40.

84. Clark, Three Types of Religious Philosophy, 64-70.

85. Ibid., 139.

86. Clark, Religion, Reason and Revelation, 196.

87. Ibid.

88. Augustine, The City of God, 22.1.

89. Geisler, Thomas Aquinas, 86.

90. Alvin C. Plantinga, God, Freedom, and Evil (Grand Rapids: Eerdmans Publishing Company, 1974), 28-31.

91. Clark, Three Types of Religious Philosophy, 139.

92. Gordon R. Lewis, Testing Christianity's Truth Claims (Lanham: University Press of America, 1990), 119.

93. Ibid., 119-120.

94. Ronald H. Nash, ed. The Philosophy of Gordon H. Clark (Philadelphia: Prebyterian and Reformed, 1968), 173-174.

95. Ibid., 173.

96. Ibid., 174.

CHAPTER FOUR:

Cornelius Van Til's Transcendental Presuppositionalism

....

Gordon Clark was not alone in his use of presuppositional apologetics. Another Calvinist scholar named Cornelius Van Til (1895-1987) also used this methodology. Despite the fact that both thinkers were presuppositionalists, they differed on many key points. Clark's presuppositionalism could be called dogmatic presuppositionalism,[1] whereas Van Til utilized what could be called transcendental presuppositionalism.[2] Still, their thought systems had much in common.

REJECTION OF TRADITIONAL APOLOGETICS

Like Clark, Van Til was opposed to traditional methods of apologetics. Van Til taught that because of man's Fall in the garden "every one of fallen man's functions operates wrongly."[3] Van Til stated that "on account of sin man is blind with respect to truth wherever truth appears."[4] Van Til taught that without the correct view about God, man cannot have the correct view of himself and the world.[5]

According to Van Til, the unsaved man is biased against God; he presupposes his own autonomy.[6] The unsaved man believes he can start with himself and find truth without aid from God. There is therefore no neutral ground between believers and nonbelievers.[7] The nonbeliever presupposes human autonomy; the believer presupposes the existence of God.

However, there is common ground: all mankind must live within God's universe.[8] All men live in the real world of reason and moral values. Because of this common ground, believers can reason with nonbelievers. Still, with the absence of neutral ground, traditional apologetics cannot even get started. People are not unbiased observers who allow the facts to determine their world view.

Instead, people interpret the facts by their preconceived world view (their presuppositions or biases).[9] Therefore, all apologetics must be by way of presupposition.[10]

Van Til disagrees with Roman Catholicism for declaring the autonomy of human reason. Roman Catholicism "ascribes ultimacy or self-sufficiency to the mind of man."[11] When Arminians, Evangelicals, and "less consistent" Calvinists defend the faith, they take the side of the Roman Church by assuming the mind of the unsaved man can of itself rise to a proper understanding of the Triune God.[12] Only a consistent Calvinistic position rightly denies the nonbeliever the ability to reason correctly (without faulty biases). Van Til adds that traditional apologetics would never prove the existence of the Triune God of the Bible. Instead, traditional apologetics only proves the existence of a finite god.[13] Van Til states that Roman Catholicism would never desire to prove the existence of an infinite God who controls whatever comes to pass. The Roman Church, according to Van Til, wants to protect man's self-sufficiency.[14]

Van Til believed the root of the problem is found in the fact that all nonbelievers suppress their knowledge of the true God (Romans 1:18-22). Concerning the unsaved man, Van Til states that "deep down in his mind every man knows that he is a creature of God and responsible to God. Every man, at bottom, knows that he is a covenant-breaker. But every man acts as though this were not so."[15] By using traditional apologetics, believers mistakenly assume that the unsaved man honestly needs proof that the God of the Bible exists. Instead, Christians should directly confront the nonbeliever by proclaiming the gospel message from the start.[16]

According to Van Til, traditional arguments are also misguided in that they use inductive arguments for Christianity. Inductive arguments are probabilistic; they do not prove their conclusions with certainty. Therefore, traditional arguments give nonbelievers an excuse for rejecting the truth of Christianity, for if Christianity is only probably true, then it is also possibly false. Van Til believed that what was needed was not a probabilistic argument for Christianity, but an argument that proved the impossibility of the contrary. Van Til believed that his transcendental argument alone proved Christianity to be true with certainty.[17]

The traditional arguments for God's existence are therefore useless. The nonbeliever must be confronted with the gospel. Only in this direct approach will the believer find a point of contact with the nonbeliever. It should not be assumed that the nonbeliever is an honest, neutral seeker of truth.[18]

REASONING BY PRESUPPOSITION

After rejecting traditional apologetics, Van Til unveils his own method of defending the faith. He states that "a truly Protestant apologetic must therefore make its beginning from the presupposition that the Triune God . . . speaks to him with absolute authority in Scripture."[19] Now that believers stand on Christian foundations, they can see "the futility of reasoning on non-Christian foundations . . ."[20] Thus, rather than argue to the existence of the Triune God who has spoken to man through His Word, apologists must presuppose His existence.

Van Til sees no middle ground at this point. Two opposing presuppositions are competing for a person's allegiance. The nonbeliever presupposes that he himself is the final or ultimate reference point in all human thought, but the believer rightly presupposes the final or ultimate reference point in human thought to be the Triune God who speaks to man through His infallible Word.[21] There is no neutral ground here. If humans were really products of chance as the nonbeliever assumes is the case, then there would be no possibility of knowing the world, ourselves, or anything else.[22] But human thought and knowledge is possible because man is who the Bible declares him to be, a being created by God.[23]

Van Til does engage in refuting the beliefs of others. For the sake of argument, believers may "place themselves with the unbeliever on his presupposition" in order to expose the contradictions which the nonbeliever holds.[24] However, even the law of noncontradiction is not presupposed by the Christian. It is only borrowed from the nonbeliever's system of thought and used by the Christian to show the internal inconsistencies of the anti-Christian thought.

In Van Til's apologetic system, only the "Triune God revealed in Scripture" is presupposed.[25] Not even nature or the laws of logic are presupposed. For man to start with himself rather than with God would be to deny his utter dependence on God. One cannot argue for

Christianity. Instead, the validity of the gospel must be presupposed. However, Van Til will allow believers to utilize the presuppositions of nonbelievers in order to refute their views.

CIRCULAR REASONING

Cornelius Van Til stated that "all reasoning is, in the nature of the case, circular reasoning."[26] By this he meant that "the starting-point, the method, and the conclusion are always involved in one another."[27] In other words, when attempting to prove something, a person must first assume the conclusion to be true before proving it to be true. Van Til was claiming that every argument contains its conclusion in its initial premise.

Philosophers refer to circular reasoning as "begging the question." It has long been considered an informal fallacy by logicians. To assume what you are attempting to prove has historically been considered to be an illegitimate form of argumentation. Most believers and nonbelievers agree on this point.

It is interesting that Van Til chooses to refer to "all reasoning" as circular. The point he is stressing is that we argue from our presuppositions, not to them.[28] Apart from regeneration by the Holy Spirit, a person will not presuppose the truth of Christianity.[29] Here, Van Til's Calvinism is evident.

PARADOX

Van Til does not believe that the law of contradiction can be found in God's being.[30] Whereas Gordon Clark viewed this law as an expression of God's very being, Van Til considers this law a human limitation that does not apply to God. He believed that Clark, and those who agree with him, make God subject to a human law. Van Til warns that the rational man will allow his reason to sit in judgment over God's Word. He will not allow the Bible to rule his life.[31]

Van Til goes so far as to speak of God's Word as seemingly contradicting itself. Though he states that God does not actually contradict Himself, he adds that God's communication to man often appears contradictory to finite human minds.[32] But, Van Til cannot have it both ways. Either God cannot contradict Himself and the law of contradiction flows from His nature, or God can contradict

Himself and the law is merely a human limitation.

If by paradox Van Til simply means an apparent contradiction, then even Clark would agree with his premise. Therefore, any criticism that Van Til made of Clark on this point would also apply to Van Til himself. However, if his usage of the term paradox does mean an actual contradiction, then nothing could be known of God. For God could both love mankind and not love mankind at the same time and in the same sense. It seems that Van Til should have withdrawn his criticism of Clark in this area and admitted that the law of contradiction flows naturally from God's being.

THE TRANSCENDENTAL ARGUMENT

Though Van Til rejected traditional apologetics, he was willing to do more than refute the nonbeliever's world view. Van Til was willing to use one argument for the truth of Christianity. He believed it to be the only valid argument for the true God. He called this argument the transcendental argument.

The transcendental argument attempts to uncover the hidden presuppositions of the nonbeliever. These hidden presuppositions are the necessary preconditions for human thought.[33] Van Til argued that all human thought and moral judgments would be impossible if the Christian God did not exist. Van Til claimed that if God did not exist, then man would know nothing. Even for man to be conscious of his own existence presupposes a consciousness of God's existence. When a nonbeliever argues against God's existence, he must first presuppose God's existence just to argue at all.[34]

For the sake of argument, a believer can place himself within the unbeliever's world view to show that the unbeliever has to presuppose the truth of Christianity just to raise an objection against Christianity.[35] Only Christianity justifies man's ability to reason. Only Christianity gives meaning to life. All other world views lead to irrationality and chaos.[36] In fact, scientific induction makes no sense in a universe without God, for only the Christian God guarantees the uniformity and order of nature necessary for scientists to argue from the particulars of nature to general conclusions about the world in which he lives.[37]

COMPARISON WITH GORDON CLARK

When comparing the thought of Cornelius Van Til with that of Gordon Clark, one finds several points of agreement as well as several areas of disagreement. First, some points of agreement between these two men will be examined.

Both were serious and consistent Calvinists. Because they both believed that no one could freely choose Christ apart from the Holy Spirit's regenerating work, direct attempts to persuade nonbelievers were thought to be counterproductive.

Both agreed that the gospel should be presupposed and not argued for. Van Til and Clark felt that to defend the truth of the gospel was to deny the Calvinist doctrine of the total depravity of man. They both believed that man's reason was damaged due to the Fall and that direct argumentation for the truth of Christianity would be useless. Still, both were willing to refute the beliefs of the nonbeliever and provide indirect confirmation for the truth of Christianity.

Both agreed that secular philosophy was a complete failure. Clark taught that all non-Christian philosophy eventually reduced to skepticism. Van Til believed that secular philosophy was futile since human reason was fallen. In his view, without presupposing the God of the Bible, no knowledge was attainable. However, Van Til believed that even nonbelievers presuppose God's existence (though they suppress this truth) in order to find truth.

Both agreed that traditional apologetics is unbiblical and useless. Throughout their writings, Clark and Van Til belittled the traditional method of defending the faith. They believed that there was no neutral battle ground between the believer and nonbeliever where Christianity could be defended. The gospel was to be presupposed rather than defended. They saw no use for the classical arguments for God's existence or for traditional usage of historical evidences for the Christian Faith.

Besides these points of agreement between Clark and Van Til, there were areas of disagreement. The following examples will illustrate this.

They disagreed about circular reasoning. Van Til believed that all reasoning is circular. The conclusion of one's arguments can always be found in one's premises. However, Clark was more rationalistic in his thinking. He considered circular reasoning a logical fallacy. Because of this, Clark dogmatically presupposed his first principle (the existence of the God of the Bible) and then deduced his beliefs from this first principle.

They disagreed about the status and use of the law of contradiction. Clark believed that the law of contradiction flowed from God's nature. He taught that God is logic. Therefore, when he presupposed the Triune God who revealed Himself in the Bible, he also presupposed the law of contradiction. He would then use this law to destroy the belief systems of nonbelievers.

Van Til, however, believed this law to be a human limitation which Clark forced upon God. Van Til believed that Clark had subjected God to this law. Though Van Til would use this law to refute other belief systems, it was only because he chose to use the "enemy's own ammunition to defeat the enemy in battle." In fact, Clark's view of the law of noncontradiction is probably what caused the widest gap between the thought of these two men. Clark presupposed the law of noncontradiction when doing apologetics. Van Til refused to do so.

STRENGTHS OF VAN TIL'S SYSTEM

In the presuppositional apologetics of Cornelius Van Til there is much to be commended. The following examples will make this clear.

He stresses the sinfulness of man. Too often, defenders of the faith tend to de-emphasize the effects of the Fall on mankind. But this is not true of Van Til. If Van Til can be accused of any fault in this area, it would be overkill. For, due to his Calvinism, man is not free to accept Christ; regeneration precedes faith.

He stresses man's suppression of God's truth. Many apologists assume that the reason why nonbelievers do not come to Christ is merely an intellectual one. Van Til rightly shows that men willfully suppress whatever knowledge of the true God they have. Van Til is correct in his view that the problem is ultimately that of a moral choice rather than an intellectual one. God has proven his existence to all men through His visible creation (Romans 1:18-22). Therefore, man has no excuse for rejecting Him.

He stresses God's work in salvation. Even non-Calvinists should commend Van Til for his focus on God's work in salvation. Apart from God's grace, no man would be saved. Traditional apologists often imply that they can lead people to Christ through argumentation alone. More emphasis is needed on the inward persuasion of the Holy Spirit concerning those to whom apologists witness. God can use traditional argumentation. Still, it is God who does the saving. The apologist can remove intellectual stumbling blocks to the faith, but only God can persuade one to turn to Christ.

He stresses the importance of faith over reason. Van Til emphasizes that one must believe in Christ to be saved. Without Christ, even the wisest man in the world will be eternally lost. Though traditional apologists are right in that man can reason to the true faith (Van Til disagrees with this), once a person through reason finds the true faith, he must submit his reason to it.

He is willing to tear down the belief systems of those who oppose the gospel and use an indirect argument for Christianity. If it were not for this point, Van Til would probably be classified as a fideist. Though he rejects traditional apologetics (like the fideist), he is willing to refute non-Christian views and give one argument for his beliefs (unlike the fideist). Van Til's transcendental argument goes beyond refuting non-Christian world views; it presents positive evidence for the Christian faith. Still, it does so in an indirect manner, rather than in the direct fashion found in traditional apologetics.

WEAKNESSES OF VAN TIL'S SYSTEM

Despite the many good things that could be said about Van Til's apologetics, there are many weaknesses in his thought. A few of these weaknesses are mentioned below.

He denies that man has the ability to test revelation-claims. Given Van Til's system, there seems to be no way to decide whether the Bible or the Koran is the Word of God. Yet the Bible frequently commands us to test the spirits, the prophets, and the messages they proclaim (1 John 4:1; Deuteronomy 18:20-22; Matthew 7:15-23; Galatians 1:8-9).[38] Also, God provided ample evidence for His revelation-claims by performing miracles through His spokesmen and by raising Jesus from the dead (Jn 20:30-31; 1 Cor

15:3-8). It seems that God has given even fallen man the ability to test revelation-claims. Whether or not man uses this ability wisely is another question. Again, Van Til's Calvinism can be seen. For without regeneration by the Holy Spirit, no one will accept the Bible as God's Word.

His view that all reasoning is circular. It is true that much of Van Til's thought is circular. It is not true that all thought is circular. Even though all men have presuppositions, they can be tested just as scientific hypotheses are tested. One does not have to sneak one's presuppositions into the premises of one's arguments. Any argument that uses circular reasoning is fallacious, regardless of whether or not the conclusion is true.

His rejection of the law of noncontradiction being universally valid. Though Van Til claimed that he only used the law of noncontradiction for the sake of argument when he shared his faith with nonbelievers, he often criticized many of his colleagues for being inconsistent Calvinists.[39] Though Van Til implied that this law is a man-made principle (or, at least only applicable to man and not to God), he diligently labored to keep his system free from contradictions. Van Til should have realized that there could be no thought or communication whatsoever without the law of contradiction. Even God cannot contradict Himself. And, since God is not subject to anything outside Himself, Clark was right to view this law as naturally flowing from God's being.

Van Til's transcendental argument is not the only valid argument for Christianity. Even John Frame, a former student of Van Til, saw problems with Van Til's transcendental argument.[40] Although Frame recognized the worth of this argument for apologetics, he did not believe it was the only valid argument for Christianity.

First, Frame doubts that the transcendental argument could be persuasive without "the help of subsidiary arguments of a more traditional kind."[41] Second, Frame thinks Van Til was wrong in his assertion that the traditional arguments proved something less than the God of the Bible.[42] Third, Frame believes that some traditional arguments often work despite the fact that the traditional apologist might wrongly assume that their arguments do not themselves presuppose a Christian world view.[43] Fourth, Frame doubts that the whole of the Christian faith can be established by a single argument which stands alone.[44] Fifth, if Van Til is right in his claim that the apologist must prove the whole biblical doctrine of God rather than just one or a few of His attributes, then the transcendental argument also fails. For the God of the Bible is more than the source of meaning, morality, and rationality. Even the transcendental argument must be supplemented by other arguments.[45] And, sixth, Frame believes that any argument (including the transcendental argument) can be rejected. Hence, further argumentation may be needed to defend the original argument.[46] Therefore, though the transcendental argument of Van Til may be a good argument for the God of the Bible, it is not the only good argument for the God of the Bible. The traditional arguments (cosmological, teleological, moral) for God's existence may also be used by the apologist.

His rejection of traditional apologetics. Finally, Van Til was wrong to reject traditional apologetics. The Bible commands believers to defend the faith (1 Peter 3:15; Colossians 4:5-6). The apostles used historical evidences to lead others to Christ (1 Corinthians 15:3-8). Even Van Til admits that man suppresses the truth that God has given him in nature (Romans 1:18-22). If this is the case, then why shouldn't apologists use traditional arguments to attempt to dislodge these truths from the nonbelievers' subconscious mind? As the last chapter showed, traditional apologetics is on much more solid ground than the presuppositional apologetics of either Van Til or Clark would admit.

ENDNOTES

1. Gordon H. Clark, Three Types of Religious Philosophy, 115-142.

2. John M. Frame, Apologetics to the Glory of God (Phillipsburg: Presbyterian and Reformed Publishing, 1994), 69-75.

3. Cornelius Van Til, Christian Apologetics (Phillipsburg: Presbyterian and Reformed Publishing Co., 1976), 43.

4. Ibid., 42.

5. Cornelius Van Til, The Defense of the Faith (Phillipsburg: Presbyterian and Reformed Publishing Co., 1967), 73.

6. Ibid., 34.

7. Ibid., 298.

8. Ibid.

9. Gordon R. Lewis, 128.

10. Van Til, Defense of the Faith, 34, 99-105, 179-180, 195, 197.

11. Ibid., 90.

12. Ibid., 78-79.

13. Ibid., 77.

14. Ibid., 78.

15. Ibid., 92, 94, 231.

16. Ibid., 94.

17. Ibid., 103.

18. Ibid., 94.

19. Ibid., 99-105, 179-180, 195, 197.

20. Ibid., 180.

21. Ibid.

22. Ibid.

23. Ibid.

24. Ibid.

25. Gordon R. Lewis, 131.

26. Van Til, The Defense of the Faith, 101.

27. Ibid.

28. Ibid.

29. Ibid., 299.

30. Ibid., 298.

31. Lewis, 133.

32. Ibid.

33. Van Til, The Defense of the Faith, 60, 150, 180, 298.

34. Frame, 69-75.

35. Van Til, The Defense of the Faith, 180.

36. Ibid.

37. Ibid.

38. Gordon R. Lewis, 144.

39. Ibid., 146.

40. Frame, 69-75.

41. Ibid., 71.

42. Ibid.

43. Ibid., 71-72.

44. Ibid., 72.

45. Ibid., 73.

46. Ibid.

CHAPTER FIVE:

The Verificational Apologetics
of Francis Schaeffer

....

Francis Schaeffer (1912-1984) was one of the twentieth century's greatest defenders of the faith. Schaeffer was a Presbyterian minister who had studied under the teachings of Cornelius Van Til. Still, Schaeffer developed his own unique way to defend the faith. Though he greatly respected his old professor, he was not a Van Tillian presuppositionalist.

In 1955, Schaeffer and his wife Edith started L'Abri ("the Shelter") in Switzerland. L'Abri became a place where intellectual drop outs could come and find a loving community, and search for meaning in life. The Schaeffer's loved their visitors enough to listen to their questions and provided these people with Christian answers in terms that "modern man" could understand.

Though Schaeffer emphasized rationally defending the faith, he knew that the ultimate apologetic (the defense of the faith) was a loving, caring Christian community. Schaeffer took seriously the words of the Lord Jesus Christ: "By this all men will know that you are My disciples, if you love one another" (John 13:35). Schaeffer believed we must proclaim the truth, but he emphasized that we must "speak the truth in love" (Ephesians 4:15).

The Schaeffer's genuinely loved people—they opened up their lives and their home to them. They cared enough for people to spend time with them and to answer their difficult questions. Francis Schaeffer had the ability to rationally defend the Christian world view. But, he and his wife also created a genuine sense of Christian community at L'Abri. This caused many of their visitors to see the reality of God's love displayed in the lives of the Schaeffer's.

SCHAEFFER'S APOLOGETIC METHODOLOGY
The line of despair. Francis Schaeffer argued that contemporary man

had fallen below what he called "the line of despair."[1] By this he meant that contemporary man has given up any hope of ever finding absolute truth, absolute morality, or meaning in life. Schaeffer identified three thinkers whose ideas led to this loss of absolutes: Immanuel Kant (1724-1804), Georg Wilhelm Friedrich Hegel (1770-1831), and Soren Kierkegaard (1813-1855).

Immanuel Kant argued that we can know reality as it appears to us (phenomena), not reality as it is (noumena).[2] Mind cannot bridge the gap between the two realms. The a priori categories of the mind read order into reality, not an order that is already there. Hence, according to Kant, man cannot know reality as it is. When one begins with unaided human reason, the phenomena and the noumena never meet. At this point, according to Schaeffer, secular philosophers gave up their attempt to find "a unified rationalistic circle that would contain all thought, and in which they could live."[3] In short, Kant's philosophical views led to modern man's skepticism in reference to knowing reality as it is.

The next thinker emphasized by Schaeffer was Hegel. Before him, philosophers for thousands of years had attempted to find truth based on antithesis. This meant that they held to the idea of absolute truth. Something could not be both true and not true at the same time and in the same sense. But Kant had shown that unaided human reason within the boundaries of antithesis led to skepticism about the real world. Hegel therefore concluded that man must try a new method. He recommended abandoning absolutes. His dialectical approach allowed for the synthesizing of contradictory statements.[4] Hegel defined truth as the unfolding world process. History unfolds in the form of a thesis which is opposed by its contrary— the antithesis. The thesis and antithesis are eventually synthesized to produce a new truth.[5] Before Hegel, the thesis was viewed as true, while the antithesis was considered false. Now, due to Hegel's influence, many believe that two contradictory statements can be synthesized. Hence, the law of noncontradiction (A cannot equal non-A at the same time and in the same way) is denied. This shift in the concept of truth from antithesis (absolute truth) to synthesis (truth is relative) resulted, according to Schaeffer, in modern man's new way of viewing reality.[6] At this point, modern man faced great despair. For there is no longer any hope of man finding truth or genuine meaning in life. There are no absolutes—truth is relative.

Schaeffer then discussed the thought of Soren Kierkegaard. With the rejection of absolutes, modern man was left without truth or meaning in life. Despair seemed to be the only alternative. But this is where Kierkegaard enters the scene. Schaeffer states that Kierkegaard realized that "Man has no meaning, no purpose, no significance" in the rational realm. There is only pessimism concerning man as man." But if man takes a leap of blind faith into the non-rational realm, says Kierkegaard, this non-reasonable faith gives man optimism.[7]

Kierkegaard emphasized the subjective nature of truth and de-emphasized the objective nature of truth. He believed that meaning, truth, and values cannot be found in the realm of reason. Hence, to find meaning, truth, and values we must take a leap of blind faith into the nonrational realm. Kierkegaard argued that truth is found by a passionate act of the will, and not through reason.[8]

The modern disciples of Kierkegaard are often called "existentialists." Atheistic existentialists (as opposed to religious existentialists like Kierkegaard) believe that life is absurd, and that, if man is to have meaning, he must create meaning for his life. The French philosopher Jean-Paul Sartre was an example of this form of atheistic existentialism. But, Schaeffer understood that not all modern men would be able to take this non-rational leap to create meaning for themselves. The result for many modern people is nihilism—the view that everything is meaningless and chaotic; life is absurd. Nihilism results in despair. And, the inevitable result of nihilistic despair is suicide. Schaeffer believed the Christian must show the optimistic existentialists that their optimism is unfounded—at least the nihilist courageously faces the consequence of a world without God. The nihilist understands that if there is no God, then man has no meaning. Life is absurd. But, we must not leave modern man in his misery and despair; we must show modern man that Christianity has the answers that give life meaning.[9]

According to Schaeffer, the influence of these three thinkers (Kant, Hegel, and Kierkegaard) has caused contemporary man to either deny the reality of absolute truths or at least give up the search for absolute truths. The places man below "the line of despair." The only option for modern man, if he desires to move above the line of despair, is through a Kierkegaardian non-rational leap in order to find truth, morality, and meaning. If Schaeffer is correct in his assessment of contemporary man, then the Christian must defend the concept of absolute truth before proclaiming the gospel, for the gospel is "true truth," (i.e., true in the traditional sense; absolutely true; true for all people, at all times, in all places). The gospel is not merely true in a subjective sense (i.e., true for me, but not true for you).

Schaeffer believed the denial of meaning and absolute truth has moved from philosophy into the arts (i.e., art, music, film, etc.). From the arts, this rejection of truth and meaning has spread to the general public. Once embraced by the culture, theology then becomes infected. Schaeffer lamented that theologians did not lead culture; instead, theologians often follow cultural trends rather than provide society with the real answers—Christian answers.[10]

Schaeffer pointed out that some non-Christian thinkers (i.e., Aldous Huxley and Timothy Leary) believed they needed to artificially induce their existential leaps through the use of hallucinigenic drugs such as LSD. These thinkers influenced an entire generation of young people by producing the counter culture in America. Many young people turned to drugs as they searched for meaning in the non-rational realm.[11] Schaeffer made his point: ideas have consequences. And, the consequences of bad ideas have the potential to destroy a culture.

Schaeffer's critique also seems to apply to postmodern thinkers. Postmodernism denies absolute truth and absolute morality. In fact, man is dead in postmodern thought, for the individual is swallowed up in his community and defined by his community's narrative. With reason and truth discarded, all that is left are stories. Each community gathers around its narrative. The narrative functions as if it were true, but it is only "true" to the community. In fact, Schaeffer's critique of secular thought may directly apply to postmodernism. If one replaces the existentialist's leap of faith with a postmodern community's narrative, then Schaeffer's assessment is on target.

Whatever the case, Schaeffer sees modern man (or what we might today call postmodern man) as facing a choice between despair and a non-rational, false hope. Schaeffer's method of evangelizing modern man is to show him that he must reason with absolutes; for the only way to deny absolutes is to assume there are absolutes.[12] The Kierkegaardian leap into the non-rational realm is therefore not an option. If modern man refuses to turn to the God of the Bible, he is damned to a meaningless life of despair (that is, if he has enough courage to refrain from a non-rational leap). According to Schaeffer, only when a person accepts the existence of the God of the Bible can life have true meaning. Without God, life is absurd. Without God, the reasonable man will wallow in despair. Hope for deliverance can only be found in the God of the Bible.

Man's dilemma. Francis Schaeffer states that "Anyone with sensitivity and concern for the world can see that man is in a great dilemma. Man is able both to rise to great heights and to sink to great depths of cruelty and tragedy."[13] Schaeffer speaks of the nobility of man as well the cruelty of man. Schaeffer declares, "So man stands with all his wonder and nobility, and yet also with his horrible cruelty that runs throughout the warp and woof of man's history."[14]

Schaeffer, in his attempt to explain the fact of man's nobility and cruelty, suggests that the only answer to the dilemma is the Christian answer. Man was created perfect and in God's image. But man has fallen into sin. Schaeffer states:

> In the area of morals, we have nothing of these answers except on the basis of a true, space-time, historic Fall. There was a time before the Fall, and then man turned from his proper integration point by choice; and in so doing, there was a moral discontinuity—man became abnormal.[15]

In the tradition of Pascal, Schaeffer sees Christianity as the only solution to the dilemma of man. Without the doctrines of Creation and the Fall, there would be no explanation for the greatness and wretchedness of man.

The mannishness of man. Schaeffer argued that man is unique in the universe. His personality and ability to verbalize places man above the animal kingdom. Schaeffer argued that since we are created in God's image, God can communicate propositionally to us.

Schaeffer reasoned that only a personal God could produce personal man. If we deny the existence of the personal God then we must also deny man's nobility, or else we must take a leap of blind faith to retain some value to human life.[16]

What is the purpose of man? Schaeffer believed that modern man has no answer to this question. Christianity does provide mankind was the answer: our purpose is to fellowship with the "God who is there." Only through Christ can our personal relationship with the personal God be restored.

Schaeffer also concluded that moral values (our knowledge of right and wrong) make no sense in a world without absolutes; and, absolutes only make sense in a theistic world. Apart from Christian presuppositions, man fails to distinguish reality from unreality, man from animal, and right from wrong.

According to Schaeffer, finite, fallen man cannot find certain knowledge if he autonomously begins with himself. Only in Scripture can finite man find certain, though not exhaustive, knowledge. Without God's revelation in the Bible, we have no final answers in regard to truth, morality, and epistemology (knowledge). Only Christianity offers an adequate explanation of the universe and man. The atheist may deny God's existence. Still, he must live in God's world. The atheist cannot live consistently with his world view. As Francis Schaeffer's former teacher Cornelius Van Til has said, the non-believer must live on "borrowed capital" from the Christian world view.[17]

Tests for truth. Schaeffer utilized three tests for truth in his apologetic for the Christian faith. First, for something to be true it must be non-contradictory. Second, the view must explain the phenomena in question. And third, a person must be able to live consistently with his theory. Schaeffer believed only the Christian world view passed all three of these tests.[18]

Schaeffer applied these three tests for truth to the possible answers for existence. The possible explanations are as follows: 1) everything came from nothing without a cause, 2) everything had an impersonal start, 3) everything is an illusion, and 4) everything had a personal start. Schaeffer argued that the first explanation is absurd for it is not possible to get something from nothing without a cause. But the second option (everything had an impersonal start) is also a faulty explanation since "the impersonal plus time plus chance" could not produce personal man—this goes against all experience. The third option is ruled out since man cannot live consistently with the assertion that everything is an illusion. Only the fourth option— that everything had a personal start—makes sense and adequately explains the mannishness of man—human personality. This fourth option is non-contradictory, it explains the data in question, and it is livable. Only the Christian answer makes sense—everything had a personal start. The infinite/personal/rational God exists and He is the cause of all else that exists.[19]

Schaeffer's method of evangelism. Francis Schaeffer developed his own method of evangelizing others. He recognized the importance of pre-evangelism when witnessing to modern man. No longer could a person be expected to come to Christ merely because of what the Bible says. The culture had become "post-Christian." To reach modern man we must dialogue with him to find out what his world view is. We must start where the nonbeliever is and bring his thought to its logical conclusion. This will leave the person with a decision: wallow in despair because life is without meaning or be open to the Christian world view. Some will choose to take the non-rational leap. Schaeffer would then show them the folly of their leap and then ask them to face despair as the logical outcome of their world view. Schaeffer called this "taking the roof off" of the person's world view.[20] Schaeffer did not believe we should allow people to feel comfortable in their unbelief. He believed we should show them that their leap is irrational and their despair is unbearable. Only embracing the Christian world view will free a person from despair or irrationalism. Only Jesus can provide true meaning in life.

Schaeffer gave two memorable examples of the inconsistency of trying to live consistently with a non-Christian world view. The first example was existentialist musician John Cage. The second was a Hindu college student.

John Cage attempted to apply his chance view of the universe to his composing of songs. He would flip a coin to determine the next note of his composition. When the orchestra would play his songs, the audience would boo loudly at the chance compositions. Cage's ultimate creation was his song entitled "four minutes and thirty-three seconds." When "playing" this song, Cage would merely sit at his piano and watch a stop watch tick away four minutes and thirty-three seconds. He would then stand and bow before the booing crowd. In Cage's world view, there is no distinction between music and non-music—everything is the product of chance and completely without meaning. Schaeffer points out that Cage was often bothered by the fact that he could not live consistently with his chance view of the universe when engaging in his favorite hobby—the eating of mushrooms. For, Cage understood that he had to ignore his chance view of reality in order to differentiate between poisonous and non-poisonous mushrooms before eating them. If Cage applied his chance view of reality to his eating of mushrooms, then Cage would no longer be alive! Even John Cage had to live as if the world is not a product of chance; even John Cage had to live as if Christianity is true.[21]

Schaeffer also wrote about a Hindu college student who was unable to live consistently with his Eastern religious view of reality. Schaeffer was lecturing to college students in a dorm when he stated that there is absolute right and wrong. The Hindu student disagreed. He stated that there is no distinction between cruelty and non-cruelty. Just then another student heard the tea pot whistling. The student grabbed the pot of boiling water and held it over the head of the Hindu student. The Hindu student asked what the other student was doing. The other student replied, "There's no difference between cruelty and non-cruelty." At that point, rather than admit that he could not live consistently with his Eastern world view, the Hindu student walked out into the night.[22]

The final apologetic. Though Schaeffer was willing to reason with people to show them the contradictions and non-livability of their false world views, He realized that the ultimate defense of the faith was not to be found in the realm of reason. Instead, it could only be found in the realm of love. Jesus said, "The World will know that you are my disciples when you have love for one another" (John 13:35). The final apologetic is a loving, Christian community.[23] Modern man longs for a loving community. At L'Abri, that loving, Christian community could be found.

SCHAEFFER'S MISUNDERSTANDING OF KEY THINKERS

Though Francis Schaeffer's apologetic methodology is an effective way to defend the faith, trained philosophers have identified several thinkers whose thought Schaeffer misrepresented. Although Schaeffer did not fully understand the beliefs of these key thinkers, he was still very perceptive about identifying trends in the thought of "modern man." Still, we must clear up the confusion Schaeffer caused by misunderstanding the key ideas of important thinkers.

Schaeffer mistakenly blamed Aquinas for the rise of secular thought. Schaeffer acted as if Thomas Aquinas was the cause of modernistic/humanistic thought.[24] Modern man thinks he does not need a word from God; divine revelation is not needed. But, this arrogance is nowhere to be found in Thomistic thought. However, the opposite is more likely to be true. Aquinas provided Christian thinkers with a thorough defense of the faith that is able to withstand the modernistic assault on Christianity, even though Aquinas predated modernism by several centuries. Also, Aquinas did not promote the idea that man could find all truth and solve all his problems through unaided human reason. This autonomous view of man finds its source in the thought of Rene Descartes, not Aquinas. Descartes' epistemological starting point "I think therefore I am" is the starting point of modern thought. On the other hand, Aquinas drew a clear distinction between truths of reason and truths of faith. Truths of reason could be proved by unaided human reason. However, truths of faith could only be attained through trust in the authority of God's Word. In short, Aquinas did not believe we could find all truth through reason alone—his philosophy placed great trust in God. Therefore, contrary to what Schaeffer taught, Aquinas cannot be blamed for the rise of autonomous, modern thought.[25] In fact, Schaeffer's argument for God from personality is somewhat similar to the way Aquinas argued for God. It appears that Schaeffer learned his mistaken and inaccurate ideas about Aquinas from his old professor Cornelius Van Til.

He misunderstood the Hegelian dialectic. Schaeffer was too quick to blame Hegel for the epistemological relativism (i.e., denial of absolute truth) we see in much of contemporary thought. Though Hegel's views were incompatible with traditional Christianity, he did not deny absolute truth altogether (as Schaeffer implies). Hegel's idealism denied the contemporary view that all truth is relative to the observer. Instead, Hegel believed that all beliefs fall short of absolute truth, and that history is an unfolding process which will produce absolute truth. Today's epistemological relativists are of a much different sort than Hegel.[26] Schaeffer oversimplifies the history of philosophy by arguing for a direct connection when there is none.

He misrepresented Kierkegaard's views. Many Christian scholars, (i.e., Clark Pinnock, C. Stephen Evans, and Ronald W. Ruegsegger, etc.) believe Schaeffer misrepresents the thought of Kierkegaard.[27] Though Kierkegaard did emphasize the volitional and existential aspects of true faith, he was not an irrationalist. Many contemporary Christian thinkers do not believe that Kierkegaard was a theological liberal or an irrationalist. They understand Kierkegaard to be emphasizing the fact that true saving faith involves an act of the will, not merely intellectual assent to correct doctrines. Though Kierkegaard was not a traditional apologist (he did not rationally provide evidences for Christianity), he was not anti-reason, nor should he be understood as denying the central truths of the Christian Faith. He was merely putting a much needed focus on the place of the will in the Christian walk. Later existentialists who threw out propositional truth altogether should not be considered the direct descendants of Kierkegaardian thought.

Schaeffer's apologetic methodology, despite these misunderstandings, has lasting value. Even though Schaeffer misunderstood many of the thinkers he discussed, his apologetic method does not lose any force. Though he may have misdiagnosed the causes of certain aspects of modern thought, he rightly understood what modern, post-Christian thought espouses. And, he presented a strong case for the truth of the Christian world view as well as an excellent refutation of modern thought. Though we should not follow Schaeffer in his misreading of the ideas of these great thinkers, we should not discard the general outline of Schaeffer's apologetic methodology. It is a defense of the faith that can be used effectively in our day. Francis Schaeffer was definitely not a trained historian of philosophical thought. Still, he understood the way contemporary man thinks, and he communicated and defended the gospel in such a way that many contemporary thinkers found attractive. We should not dispose of Schaeffer's unique and effective apologetic approach merely because of his lack of philosophical sophistication.

SCHAEFFER'S CULTURAL APOLOGETICS

Francis Schaeffer proclaimed that Western culture is now in a "post-Christian era." By this he meant the same thing Nietzsche meant when he declared "God is dead." Schaeffer was saying that the Christian world view was no longer the dominant presupposition of Western culture. Now, a secular humanistic view of reality permeates the thought of the West.[28] Due to this change in world view, modern man has fallen below what Schaeffer called "the line of despair."[29] Schaeffer meant that, by throwing the God of the Bible out of the equation, modern man, left to himself and without divine revelation, could not find absolute truth and eventually gave up his search for it. According to Schaeffer, modern man no longer thinks in terms of antithesis (i.e., the law of non-contradiction); he now views truth as relative. And, since he believes there are no absolutes, modern man has rejected universal moral laws and has embraced moral relativism.

Schaeffer wrote concerning America, "our society now functions with no fixed ethics," and "a small group of people decide arbitrarily what, from their viewpoint, is for the good of society at that precise moment and they make it law."[30] Schaeffer compares this present climate of arbitrary lawmaking to the fall of the Roman Empire. The finite gods of Rome where not sufficient to give a base in law for moral absolutes; therefore, the Roman laws were lax and promoted self-interest rather than social harmony. This eventually led to a state of social anarchy as violence and promiscuity spread throughout the empire. To keep order, the Roman Empire had to become increasingly more authoritative. Due to Rome's oppressive control over its people, few Romans believed their culture was worth saving when the barbarian invasions began.[31] Schaeffer saw that America, like ancient Rome, had turned to arbitrary laws which have led to an increase in crime and promiscuity, which in turn has led to ever-increasing government control. Schaeffer stated this principle as follows:

The humanists push for "freedom," but having no Christian consensus to contain it, that "freedom" leads to chaos or to slavery under the state (or under an elite). Humanism, with its lack of any final base for values or law, always leads to chaos. It then naturally leads to some form of authoritarianism to control the chaos. Having produced the sickness, humanism gives more of the same kind of medicine for the cure. With its mistaken concept of final reality, it has no intrinsic reason to be interested in the individual, the human being.[32]

Schaeffer also noted that most American leaders no longer consider themselves subject to God's laws. They often view themselves as answerable to no one. They do not acknowledge "inalienable rights" given to each individual by God. Instead, American leaders play God by distributing "rights" to individuals and by making their own arbitrary laws. Schaeffer quotes William Penn who said, "If we are not governed by God, then we will be ruled by tyrants."[33]

Schaeffer saw the 1973 legalization of abortion as a by-product of man playing God by legislating arbitrary laws and by the few forcing their will on the many.[34] But, according to Schaeffer, this is just the beginning, for once human life has been devalued at one stage (i.e., the pre-birth stage), then no stage of human life is safe. Abortion will lead to infanticide (the murdering of babies already born) and euthanasia (so called "mercy-killing").[35] Christianity teaches that human life is sacred because man was created in God's image, but now that modern man has rejected the Christian world view (the death of God), the death of man will follow (unless modern man repents) and man will be treated as non-man.

Schaeffer documents the erosion of respect for human life in the statements of Nobel Prize winners Watson and Crick. These two scientists, after winning the Nobel Prize for cracking the genetic code, publicly recommended that we should terminate the lives of infants, three days old and younger, if they do not meet our expectations.[36]

In his response to behavioral scientist B. F. Skinner's book Beyond Freedom and Dignity, Schaeffer argued that Western culture's rejection of God, truth, and God's moral laws will lead to the death of man. Written in 1971, Skinner's book proposed a "utopian" society ruled by a small group of intellectual elitists who control the environment and genetic makeup of the masses. Schaeffer stated, "We are on the verge of the largest revolution the world has ever known—the control and shaping of men through the abuse of genetic knowledge, and chemical and psychological conditioning."[37] Schaeffer referred to Skinner's utopian proposals as "the death of man,"[38] and wrote concerning Skinner's low view of C. S. Lewis:

> Twice Skinner specifically attacked C. S. Lewis. Why? Because he is a Christian and writes in the tradition of the literatures of freedom and dignity. You will notice that he does not attack the evangelical church, probably because he doesn't think it's a threat to him. Unhappily, he is largely right about this. Many of us are too sleepy to be a threat in the battle of tomorrow. But he understands that a man like C. S. Lewis, who writes literature which stirs men, is indeed a threat.[39]

Schaeffer understood not only the failure of secular humanism, but he also realized that Eastern pantheism offered no escape from the death of man. Only a return to the Christian world view could save the West from the death of man. He stated:

> Society can have no stability on this Eastern world-view or its present Western counterpart. It just does not work. And so one finds a gravitation toward some form of authoritarian government, an individual tyrant or group of tyrants who takes the reins of power and rule. And the freedoms, the sorts of freedoms we have enjoyed in the West, are lost. We are, then, brought back to our starting point. The inhumanities and the growing loss of freedoms in the West are the result of a world-view which has no place for "people." Modern humanistic materialism is an impersonal system. The East is no different. Both begin and end with impersonality.[40]

Schaeffer called upon evangelicals to sound the alarm, warning the church and society to repent, for the death of man is approaching:

> Learning from the mistakes of the past, let us raise a testimony that may still turn both the churches and society around—for the salvation of souls, the building of God's people, and at least the slowing down of the slide toward a totally humanistic society and an authoritarian suppressive state.[41]

CLASSIFYING SCHAEFFER'S METHOD OF APOLOGETICS

Francis Schaeffer was neither a presuppositionalist nor a classical apologist. It would probably be best to classify him as a verificationalist. Schaeffer was not a presuppositionalist in that his "presupposition" of the existence of the Christian God functioned more like a hypothesis—it could be verified or falsified. Whereas presuppositionalists like Cornelius Van Til and Gordon Clark started with the Triune God and argued from Him to everything else, Schaeffer was willing to test his God hypothesis. Van Til and Clark never allowed their presupposition to be tested.

Schaeffer was also not a classical apologist. He never used traditional arguments for God. He refused to argue from something to God. Instead, he started with the hypothesis of the Triune God who revealed Himself in Scripture and then put this hypothesis to the test. Schaeffer was willing to have his so-called presupposition tested or verified. Still, he did not argue from created things to God (although his argument for God from personality does seem to go against the main flow of Schaeffer's thought). Rather, he argued that the Christian explanation or hypothesis is the only explanation that explains the data in question and gives meaning to life.

Hence, Schaeffer is neither presuppositionalist nor a classical apologist. Instead, he is a verificational apologist. Verificationalism is something akin to a half-way house between presuppositionalism and classical apologetics.

It should also be added that Schaeffer not only used his verificational approach in his defense the faith, but he was also willing to utilize cultural apologetics to argue for the truth of Christianity.

As a cultural apologist, Schaeffer argued that Western civilization's rejection of the Christian world view has led to a destructive influence in our societies. And, reasoned Schaeffer, only a return to the Christian world view can reverse this dangerous trend.

Schaeffer's unique method of defending the faith should not be ignored. Despite the oversimplifications and misunderstandings in his thought, there is much apologetic ammunition to be found in the thought of Francis Schaeffer. His apologetic method can be used today with great success.

ENDNOTES

1. Francis A. Schaeffer, The Complete Works of Francis A. Schaeffer, vol. 1. (Westchester: Crossway Books, 1982), 8.

2. Ibid., vol. 5, 177-178.

3. Ibid., vol. 5, 178., vol. 1. 10.

4. Ibid., vol. 1, 232-233.

5. Ibid., vol. 1, 13-14.

6. Ibid., 10.

7. Ibid., 238.

8. Ibid., 14-16.

9. Ibid., 57-59, 140-141.

10. Ibid., 54.

11. Ibid., 22-23.

12. Ibid., 229.

13. Ibid., 109.

14. Ibid., 293.

15. Ibid., 304.

16. Ibid., 119-122.

17. Ibid., 323-344.

18. Ibid., 121.

19. Ibid., 280-287.

20. Ibid., 140-142.

21. Ibid., vol. 1, 77-79; vol. 5, 202-203.

22. Ibid., vol. 1, 110.

23. Ibid., 187.

24. Ibid., 209-211, 240.

25. Ronald W. Ruegsegger, ed. Reflections on Francis Schaeffer (Grand Rapids: Zondervan Publishing House, 1986), 112-115, 185-186. See also Norman L. Geisler, Thomas Aquinas: An Evangelical Appraisal (Grand Rapids: Baker Book House, 1991), 12, 57-62.

26. Ruegsegger, 115-118.

27. Ibid., 118-120, 187.

28. Francis Schaeffer, A Christian Manifesto (Westchester: Crossway Books, 1981), 17-18.

29. Francis Schaeffer, Complete Works, vol. 1, 8-11.

30. Schaeffer, A Christian Manifesto, 48.

31. Schaeffer, Complete Works, vol. 5, 85-89.

32. Schaeffer, A Christian Manifesto, 29-30.

33. Ibid., 32-34.

34. Ibid., 49.

35. Schaeffer, Complete Works, vol. 5, 317. see also vol. 4, 374.

36. Ibid., vol. 5, 319-320.

37. Ibid., vol. 1, 381.

38. Ibid., 383.

39. Ibid., 382-383.

40. Ibid., vol. 5, 381.

41. Ibid., vol. 4, 364.

CHAPTER SIX:

The Apologetic Methodology
of Walter Martin

....

During his lifetime, the late Dr. Walter Martin (1928-1989) was the world's leading authority on non-Christian cults. He earned a Master degree from New York University and a Ph.D. in comparative religions from California Coast University. He was the original "Bible Answer Man" and the founder and director of the Christian research Institute. His work The Kingdom of the Cults continues to be the standard textbook dealing with a Christian exposition and response to non-Christian cults. Walter Martin's apologetic methodology can be classified as "comparative religious apologetics."

Martin defined a cult as "a group of people gathered about a specific person or person's misinterpretation of the Bible."[1] Martin stated that "the cults contain many major deviations from historic Christianity"; yet, they still claim to be Christian.[2]

This chapter will summarize Martin's exposition and refutation of several non-Christian cults. Since most cults consider the Bible to be God's Word (though they misinterpret its contents), Martin was able to refute these cults by presenting scriptural passages that contradict their teachings. Martin dealt with numerous cults in his works; those discussed below will suffice to show how Martin did his comparative religious apologetics.

MORMONISM

Mormonism is also known as the Church of Jesus Christ of Latter-Day Saints. Joseph Smith founded this cult in New York state in the 1820's.[3] Smith moved the cult first to Ohio, then to Illinois. After Smith's death in Illinois, he was succeeded by Brigham Young, who moved his followers to Utah in the late 1840's.[4] There the cult grew to what it is today.

Mormonism has several sacred writings. The Bible is considered God's Word, so long as it has been translated correctly.[5] The Book of Mormon is supposedly an inspired account of the Hebrews who left the Holy Land for America around 589BC.[6] Smith claimed The Book of Mormon was revealed to him by an angel named Moroni.[7] The historical inaccuracies contained in the Book of Mormon are well documented.[8] Evidence has been presented indicating that a retired pastor named Solomon Spalding was the real author of The Book of Mormon.[9] Though Spalding intended this work to be a novel, Joseph Smith gained access to it after the death of Spalding and proclaimed it to be divine revelation.[10]

Doctrine and Covenants is another sacred Mormon writing. It contains most of the unique Mormon doctrines (priesthood functions, plurality of gods, eternal progression, principles of polygamy).[11] The Pearl of Great Price contains "the Book of Moses" (which deals with the first six chapters of Genesis), "the Book of Abraham" (Abraham's supposed writings while in Egypt), and the official history of the Mormon church.[12] Mormons, in addition to their sacred writings, accept the prophecies of their living prophets as authoritative revelation from God.[13]

Walter Martin clearly demonstrated that Mormon doctrines contradict the Bible in essential areas. Mormon theology denies the Christian doctrine of the Trinity. Though Mormons believe the Father, Son, and Holy Spirit are three separate Persons, they reject the Christian view that they are one God. The Latter-Day Saints teach that the Father, Son, and Holy Spirit are three separate gods.[14] This is consistent with the Mormon doctrine of the plurality of gods, the teaching that there are an infinite number of gods in existence.[15] This contradicts the biblical teaching that only one true God exists (Exodus 20:1-6; Deuteronomy 6:4; Isaiah 43:10; 44:6; 45:5-7, 14, 22; 1 Corinthians 8:4-6; 10:19-20; 1 Timothy 2:5). In a strange twist of theology the Book of Mormon teaches the doctrine of the Trinity (2 Nephi 31:21; Alma 11:44)! Still, Mormon teaching contradicts both the Bible and its own Book of Mormon by denying the doctrine of the Trinity.

Not only do Mormons teach the plurality of gods, they also believe that male Mormons can someday become gods.[16] This is called the doctrine of eternal progression. Mormon prophets have taught that God was once a man, and that He became a god; likewise, men can also become gods.[17] Martin points out that the Bible teaches that there is only one true God, and that there never were nor ever will be any other gods. God proclaims, "Before Me there was no God formed, and there will be none after Me" (Isaiah 43:10). In fact, it is not God who said that men could become gods; Satan is the originator of that lie (Genesis 3:5).

Walter Martin showed that the Mormon church proclaims a different Jesus than the Jesus of the Bible. Their Jesus is not God the second Person of the Trinity. The Mormon Jesus is one of many gods. He was not always God. In fact, the Jesus of Mormonism is getting better; He is still progressing in His godhood.[18] Again, the Latter-Day Saints are refuted by the Bible which teaches that Jesus was God from the beginning. He never became a god (John 1:1, 14), for, "Jesus Christ is the same yesterday and today, yes and forever" (Hebrews 13:8).

Mormons do not accept the Bible as the final Word of God; they add their own "sacred" books. However, the Bible declares itself to be "the faith which was once for all delivered to the saints" (Jude3). Scriptural warnings against adding to God's Word are ignored by Mormons (Proverbs 30:5-6; Revelation 22:18-19). The fullness of God's revelation to man culminated in the incarnation and ministry of Jesus (Hebrews 1:1-3). Those who knew Jesus personally (the apostles) were His authoritative witnesses (John 15:26-27; Ephesians 2:20). Any future "revelation" must be tested by the authoritative witness of the apostles. When this is done, Mormonism fails the test.

Mormonism proclaims a different salvation than that of the Bible. Salvation in Mormonism is attained by exercising faith in Jesus, plus Mormon baptism, good works, and obedience to Mormon ordinances.[19] This contradicts the Christian doctrine of salvation by God's grace alone through faith in Jesus alone (John 3:16-18; 14:6; Romans 3:10, 23; 6:23; Ephesians 2:8-9). Mormonism teaches that Jesus died so that all men would be resurrected and then judged according to their works.[20] The Bible, however, teaches that Jesus died so that all who trust in Him for salvation would receive the free gift of eternal life (John 1:29; Ephesians 1:7; 1 Peter 2:24; 3:18;

1 John 1:7). The biblical view of salvation is through the work of Christ; the Mormon view of salvation is through human effort.

Mormons believe that their church alone has the true priesthood.[21] Scripture declares that all believers are priests of God (1 Peter 2:4-5; Revelation 1:6). All true believers are called priests because they intercede on behalf of others and they offer their bodies as living sacrifices to the Lord (Romans 12:1-2). The Old Testament priesthood with all its symbols and ceremonies was fulfilled in Christ (Colossians 2:16-17; Hebrews 10:1, 10-14). Jesus is the only mediator that mankind needs (1 Timothy 2:5). People do not need the Mormon priesthood to find eternal life; people need Jesus, the true Jesus of the Bible.

The Mormon practice called baptism for the dead is unscriptural.[22] The Word of God declares that people do not get a second chance for salvation after death (Luke 16:19-31; Hebrews 9:27). Therefore, one should not be baptized for another person who has died.

Joseph Smith and Brigham Young practiced polygamy despite the fact that it was forbidden in the Bible.[23] Jesus said that, "He who created them from the beginning made them male and female . . . and the two shall become one flesh" (Matthew 19:4-5). Paul demanded that an elder or deacon must be "the husband of one wife" (1 Timothy 3:2, 12). Joseph Smith and Brigham Young were not qualified to be elders or deacons in a local church, not to mention founders of a new "Christian" religious movement. Even the Book of Mormon admits that the Old Testament saints who practiced polygamy greatly displeased the Lord (Jacob 2:24).

Obviously, Mormonism is a perversion of the Word of God. Mormonism is not the one true faith; it is a non-Christian cult. As Walter Martin has demonstrated, when Mormonism is tested against scripture, it fails miserably.

JEHOVAH'S WITNESSES
Walter Martin also refuted the Jehovah's Witnesses cult. The Jehovah's Witnesses (also known as the Watchtower Bible and Tract Society) trace their roots to Charles Taze Russell. He began to teach Bible studies in the 1870's. Though Russell was raised in a Christian home,

he thought that the scriptural teaching of eternal torment was unjust. He also believed that Christ's return would be invisible. He denied Christ's deity and bodily resurrection, as well as salvation by grace. He began to believe that his own interpretation of the Bible was the supreme authority.[24] He predicted that Armageddon would occur in 1914; this prophecy obviously failed.[25]

After Russell's death, Joseph Franklin Rutherford succeeded him as president. Rutherford retained the doctrines of Russell, and added the emphasis on "Jehovah" as the only true name for God.[26] Rutherford's predictions of Armageddon also failed in 1918 and 1925.[27]

The Jehovah's Witnesses "translated" their own version of the Bible called the New World Translation of the Bible. This translation is not supported by any reputable Greek or Hebrew scholar. In John 1:1, all recognized translations refer to Jesus as "God." But, in the Jehovah's Witnesses' translation Jesus is called "a god."[28] Other passages in the New World Translation contain questionable readings that strip Christ of His deity.[29]

Walter Martin showed that the Jehovah's Witnesses deny Christ's deity. They have become experts in explaining away scriptural passages that attribute deity to Jesus (Isaiah 9:6; Zechariah 14:5; John 1:1; 5:17-18; 8:23-24, 58; 10:30-33; 20:28; Philippians 2:5-7; Colossians 2:9; 2 Peter 1:1; Revelation 1:17-18). However, these passages do in fact teach that Jesus is God. Though Jehovah's Witnesses often sound confident when attacking these verses, their unique interpretations (or translations) of these passages lack scholarship. Downplaying Christ's deity, Jehovah's Witnesses often overemphasize passages which speak of the limitations of Christ's human nature (Matthew 24:36) and His submission to the Father in order to provide salvation for mankind (John 14:28; Philippians 2:5-8). The Watchtower interprets Colossians 1:15 and Revelation 3:14 to mean that Jesus is the first being that God created. However, the former verse actually declares Christ to be the supreme ruler over all creation since He is its Creator (Colossians 1:15-17). Revelation 3:14 declares Christ to be the origin of all creation. In other words, He is the source of all created existence.[30]

Jehovah's Witnesses also deny the Christian doctrine of the Trinity. Though the Bible teaches that there is only one God (Isaiah

43:10; 44:6), the Word of God declares that the Father is God (Galatians 1:1), the Son is God (Titus 2:13), and the Holy Spirit is God (Acts 5:3-4). The Scriptures also maintain that the Father, Son, and Holy Spirit are three distinct Persons (Matthew 3:16-17; 28:19; John 14:16, 26). Therefore, there is only one God, but this one God exists eternally as three equal Persons. This is the Christian doctrine of the Trinity. However, the Jehovah's Witnesses teach that only the Father is God. They consider Jesus to be a lesser god; He was God's first creation.[31] Jehovah's Witnesses believe that the Holy Spirit is nothing more than God's active, impersonal force.[32] However, the Bible clearly identifies the Holy Spirit as a Person. He is called "another Helper" (John 14:16), and He bears witness of Christ (John 15:26). He can be lied to (Acts 5:3-4) and grieved (Ephesians 4:30). He also speaks (Acts 8:29; 10:19; 13:2; 21:11). Though the doctrine that God is a three-Personed Being goes beyond human understanding, it is not contradictory. The doctrine of the Trinity is biblical. To deny this doctrine is to oppose the clear teaching of Scripture in this area.

The Watchtower Society denies that Jesus rose bodily from the dead. They teach that He was raised as a spirit being.[33] However, Jesus predicted that He would raise His own body from the dead (John 2:19-21). Jesus also proved He had risen bodily from the dead by showing the apostles His wounds, allowing them to touch His body, and by eating food with them (Luke 24:36-43; John 20:26-27).

Jehovah's Witnesses deny that Christ will visibly and bodily return to earth someday.[34] They believe that Jesus invisibly returned to Brooklyn, New York in 1914.[35] This contradicts the biblical teaching that Jesus' return to earth will be bodily and visible (Revelation 1:7; Matthew 24:23-31; Acts 1:9-12). Christ will return to the nation of Israel (Zechariah 14:3-5), not Brooklyn, New York. And, when Jesus returns, every eye will see Him (Revelation 1:7).

The Watchtower denies salvation by God's grace alone through faith in Jesus alone (John 3:16-18; Romans 3:10, 20-23; Ephesians 2:8-9; 1 Peter 3:18; 2 Corinthians 5:15, 21). They teach that Jesus' death removed the effects of Adam's sin on mankind so that people can now save themselves by living a righteous life until death.[36]

Jehovah's Witnesses deny the existence of the human soul. They believe that after death man ceases to exist until he is resurrected to be judged. This is called soul-sleep.[37] However, the Word of God declares that when a believer dies, he or she immediately goes to be with the Lord (Acts 7:59; Philippians 1:21-24; 2 Corinthians 5:8). The Bible also teaches that nonbelievers who die do not ceases to exist, but go immediately into conscious torment (Luke 16:19-31).

The Jehovah's Witnesses also deny the eternal, conscious torment of the wicked. They teach that annihilation is the final state of the lost.[38] However, the Word of God declares that nonbelievers will be "thrown into the lake of fire" where they will be "tormented day and night forever" (Mark 9:47-48; Revelation 14:9-11; 20:10, 15).

The Watchtower society contradicts the Word of God in many other areas as well. They refuse to salute the United States flag or fight in any war to defend this nation.[39] This disobeys the biblical commands to submit to the governing authorities and render them the honor they are due (Mark 12:17; Romans 13:1-7). Jehovah's Witnesses condemn the usage of any name for God other than "Jehovah."[40] Yet, Jesus instructed His disciples to call God "our Father" (Matthew 6:9). The Watchtower organization claims to be God's prophet,[41] but the Word of God shows their organization to be a false prophet: their prophecies have failed (Deuteronomy 18:20-22), they have produced the "bad fruit" of heresies (Matthew 7:15-23), and they have proclaimed the return of a hidden, invisible Christ—Jesus taught His return to earth would be visible to all (Matthew 24:23-27; Revelation 1:7). Therefore, their claim to be the "witnesses" of Jehovah is false.

CHRISTIAN SCIENCE

Besides the Latter-days Saints and the Jehovah's Witnesses, Walter Martin also refuted several other non-Christian cults. One is the Christian Science cult. The Christian Science cult was founded by Mary Baker Eddy in 1866.[42] Christian Science teaches that God is an impersonal force and that sin, death, pain, and sickness are illusions.[43] Christian Scientists also deny the existence of the material realm.[44] They deny that Jesus is the Christ. Instead, they view Jesus as a mere man who exercised His "Christ consciousness" to a greater extent than any other person. All people have the "divine idea" or

"Christ consciousness" within them and some exercise it better than others.[45] Salvation in Christian Science is the recognition that sin and death are illusions.[46] Jesus' death on the cross does not cleanse anyone from sin.[47]

In response to Christian Scientists, Christians must declare that God is a personal Being who can communicate with and love His creatures (Exodus 3:14; John 3:16). He is not the impersonal force proclaimed by Mary Baker Eddy. The Bible teaches that sin, death, pain, and sickness are real (1 John 1:8-10; Romans 3:23; Hebrews 9:27; Romans 6:23). Scripture relates that the material universe does exist (Genesis 1:1; Colossians 1:15-16). The Bible identifies Jesus as the Christ (1 John 5:1) and as God in the flesh (John 1:1, 14). The Word of God reveals that man can only be saved through Jesus (John 3:16-18; 14:6) and that salvation was provided when Jesus died on the cross for man's sin (1 Peter 2:24; 3:18).

THE UNITY SCHOOL OF CHRISTIANITY

The Unity School of Christianity is an offshoot of Christian Science.[48] Founded by Charles and Myrtle Fillmore, this cult teaches that man is divine; all have the "Christ-consciousness" within them.[49] Unity views Jesus as merely a man who exercised His Christ-consciousness more than any other man.[50] Sin, the devil, and eternal punishment do not exist; they are illusions.[51] Salvation in the Unity cult is through reincarnation, and everyone will eventually be saved.[52] Unlike Christian Science, the Unity School of Christianity does believe in the existence of the physical world.[53]

The teachings of the Unity cult can be refuted in much the same fashion as those of Christian Science. However, a scriptural refutation of reincarnation should be added when dealing with Unity. The Bible teaches that it is appointed for man to die once, not many times (Hebrews 9:27). The Word of God makes it clear that Jesus alone was punished for our sins (Hebrews 1:3; 1 Peter 2:24; 3:18); man does not need to be purged for his own sins through reincarnation. Jesus clearly taught that a deceased person cannot return to this world for a second chance (Luke 16:19-31).

THE UNIFICATION CHURCH

Walter Martin exposed and refuted the false teachings of the Unification Church. The Unification Church was founded in 1954 by the Reverend Sun Myung Moon.[54] Moon taught that mankind fell spiritually when Eve had sexual intercourse with Lucifer, and that mankind fell physically when Eve later had sexual intercourse with Adam.[55] Moon instructed his disciples that Jesus prematurely died, having only provided for man's spiritual salvation.[56] According to Moon, Jesus failed to provide physical salvation for mankind by raising a family who would inherit His sinless nature. He died before He could procure such a family. Now, it is up to Moon to physically save mankind.[57] Though he has never openly declared so, Moon strongly implies that He is the Lord of the second advent.[58] His cult denies the deity of Christ.[59]

When witnessing to Moon's followers, it should be pointed out that the Bible teaches that the Fall of mankind was due to disobedience of a clear command of God (Genesis 3:1-6). It had nothing to do with sex. The Scriptures teach that Jesus did not fail, and He accomplished salvation completely for mankind (1 Peter 2:24; 3:18; Hebrews 10:14; Matthew 20:28). Even the physical redemption of believers was accomplished by Christ's death, though it won't be realized until Christ's return (1 Corinthians 15:50-57; Revelation 20:1-6). People do not need Moon to save them. Jesus is the only Savior. Moon is also not the Lord of the second advent, for Jesus taught that He Himself would return to earth (John 14:1-3; Acts 1:9-11; Revelation 22:20).

THE WAY INTERNATIONAL

The Way International was founded by Victor Paul Wierwille.[60] This cult denies that Jesus is God. According to them, Jesus did not pre-exist His conception in the womb of Mary.[61] Wierwille taught the doctrines of soul-sleep and annihilation of the wicked.[62] Since sins are thought to have no detrimental effect on the human spirit once saved, repentance is seldom stressed in the cult.[63]

When confronting members of this cult, the Christian apologist must defend the deity of Christ (Isaiah 9:6; John 1:1, 14; Titus 2:13; 2 Peter 1:1) and argue for His pre-existence (John 1:1-

14; 8:58; 17:5; Colossians 1:15-17). The defender of the Christian faith should refute the concept of soul-sleep (Luke 16:19-31; 2 Corinthians 5:8) and give scriptural support for eternal conscious torment in hell (Revelation 14:9-11; 20:10, 15). Those in the Way International need to be informed that sin does effect the spiritual nature of man. God calls men and women to flee from their sinfulness (John 8:11, 31-36; 1 John 2:1; Romans 3:31; 6:14-18; 1 Corinthians 6:18; Hebrews 10:26-27).

SCIENTOLOGY

Scientology was founded by L. Ron Hubbard.[64] Scientology teaches that mankind is descended from a race of uncreated, all-powerful gods called thetans. Thetans surrendered their power in order to come to earth. They gradually evolved from non-life to life, and eventually into humans who had forgotten their own deity. Scientologists counsel others to overcome their problems by remembering their own deity.[65] This is often done through past-lives-regression therapy.[66] The deity of Christ, the sinfulness of man, and the eternal flames of hell are all denied by this cult.[67] When dealing with Scientologists, Christians should show that the belief that man is divine originated with Satan (Genesis 3:1-6). It must be pointed out that all are sinners (Romans 3:10, 23) who need Christ's salvation (John 3:16-18; 14:6). Evidence for Christ's deity and eternal conscious torment should be presented, and reincarnation should be refuted.

THE UNITARIAN UNIVERSALIST ASSOCIATION

The Unitarian Universalist Association is the result of a merger between two heretical groups.[68] The Unitarian Church denied that Jesus is God and taught that God is only one Person (the Father).[69] The Universalist Church taught that all people will ultimately be saved.[70] These two heretical movements merged in 1959.[71] This cult teaches that all religions lead to God, the Bible contains errors, and the impossibility of miracles.[72] Since this cult denies inerrancy, the best approach for the apologist to take is to use historical evidences to argue for the deity of Christ and the inspiration and inerrancy of the Bible. An apologist must also be able to provide evidence for the possibility of miracles when dealing with this cult.

THE NEW AGE MOVEMENT

Though Walter Martin died in 1989, he was already aware of the fact that eastern thought and ancient pagan ideas were becoming popular in America. Martin saw that comparative religious apologists must be able to deal with and refute the false teachings and dangerous practices of what has become known as the New Age Movement. The New Age Movement is growing rapidly in America.[73] It is probably the biggest threat Christianity faces going into the twenty-first century.[74] Therefore, Christian apologists must be able to dialogue with new agers and be able to refute their teachings.

The New Age Movement is the immersing of western culture with eastern thought.[75] It is largely responsible for the current revival of ancient occultism in the United States.[76] New Agers believe in a coming new age of spiritual enlightenment and peace towards which man is evolving.[77] New Agers seek a one world government and the destruction of nationalistic barriers between the peoples of the earth.[78] The New Age Movement is not a conscious conspiracy (on the human level) to take over the world, though its thrust towards a one world government may be demonically inspired.[79] Rather, it is a network of numerous groups who share similar beliefs and goals.[80]

History of the New Age Movement. The New Age Movement had its roots in the ancient occultism (secret arts) of Sumeria, India, Egypt, Babylon, and Persia.[81] However, its move into western culture has been fairly recent. The Theosophical Society is responsible for bringing the New Age Movement to America.[82] Founded by Helena Blavatsky in 1875, this cult promoted seances, spirit's and Hindu thought in the United States.[83] The Theosophical Society had three primary goals. First, it sought to declare the universal brotherhood of all mankind. Second, it desired to teach others the unity of all religions. Third, it encouraged others to tap into the spiritual powers within man.[84] This led to the current interest of many Americans in the New Age Movement.[85] The Theosophical Society taught that the world is awaiting many avatars (manifestations of God who reveal spiritual truth to the world).[86] Blavatsky considered Jesus, Buddha, and Mohammad to be avatars.[87]

Annie Besant and Alice Bailey were later leaders of the

Theosophical Society.[88] Their books are still popular today within new age circles.[89] Bailey claimed to have communicated with several spirit guides.[90] Her books are published through a company called "Lucius Trust," formerly known as the "Lucifer Publishing Company."[91]

American culture had been dominated by the Christian world view from about 1620 to 1860.[92] After Charles Darwin published his Origin of Species, American culture began to take on more of a secular mindset (1860-1960). Though most Americans rejected philosophical atheism (the belief that no God exists), they accepted practical atheism. In other words, they lived like no God existed. They rejected the traditional morality taught in the Bible. Moral relativism became popular. Still, Americans were not satisfied with materialistic pleasures; they longed for spiritual experiences. Even so, they did not want an authoritative God who would forbid some of their practices. This left many Americans open to eastern influences. This may also partly explain the "hippie culture" and the widespread experimentation with hallucinogenic drugs. The 1960's were famous for large-scale rebellion against materialism and authority. With many Americans starving for a religious experience, this country abandoned its secular outlook and opened the door to the occult. It was in this context that the New Age Movement became popular in America.[93]

Common New Age Beliefs. The New Age Movement is antithetical to Christianity. The New Age Movement accepts a pantheistic world view, the belief that God is the universe.[94] God is thought by New Agers to be an impersonal force.[95] Obviously this contradicts Christianity, for the Bible teaches that God is not identical to the universe; rather, God created the universe (Genesis 1:1; John 1:1-3; Colossians 1:15-17). God is therefore separate from the universe. The God of the Bible is not impersonal. He is a personal God who loves the people He has created and has communicated to them in His Word (John 3:16; 2 Timothy 3:16-17; 2 Peter 1:20-21).

New Agers teach that all humans are God since they are part of the universe (which they equate with God).[96] On the other hand, the Bible states that man is not God (1 Samuel 15:29; Ezekiel 28:1-2, 9-10; Matthew 19:25-26). In fact, the lie that humans are or can be god was originated by Satan (Genesis 3:1-7; Isaiah 14:12-

14). Since New Agers believe they are God, they see no need to be saved.[97] The Bible, however, teaches the need for all people to be saved (Romans 3:10; 23; 6:23; John 3:16-18; 14:6). New Agers refuse to acknowledge the reality of sin.[98] However, the Bible teaches that sin is real. All are sinners; all need the Savior, the Lord Jesus (Romans 3:10, 23; 1 Peter 2:24; 3:18; 1 John 1:8-10).

New Agers accept the doctrine of reincarnation.[99] Reincarnation teaches that the individual soul passes through the cycle of death and rebirth. The soul reanimates a different body (whether animal or human) after death until all negative karma is done away with. Then the individual soul is absorbed into the world soul.[100] This is in direct opposition to biblical teaching. The Bible proclaims that "it is appointed for man to die once . . ." (Hebrews 9:27). Jesus' story of Lazarus the beggar and the rich man illustrates that man does not get another chance beyond this life (Luke 16:19-31). Rather than reincarnation purging a soul from sin, Jesus alone paid for the sins of mankind (John 1:29; Hebrews 1:1-3; 1 Peter 2:24; 3:18).

Many New Agers believe the external world is merely an illusion; it does not exist.[101] Still, they live as if it does exist: they clothe and feed themselves. They do not jump off of high buildings. A belief system that cannot be consistently lived should be seriously reconsidered.

New Agers are often moral relativists. They deny there is right and wrong.[102] Obviously, the Bible disagrees for the scriptures teach absolute moral laws that are above all mankind (Exodus 20:1-17; Micah 6:8; Isaiah 5:20; 1 John 1:8-10). New Agers do not live consistently with their belief in moral relativism. They do live as though some things are wrong. They protest the production of nuclear weapons.[103] They march to save the whales, seals, and other endangered species.[104] They are determined to save the earth from global warming.[105] Though most New Agers deny the existence of universal moral values, they clearly judge certain things as being "wrong." If New Agers were consistent with their moral relativistic leanings, then they could not even judge the barbarous actions of Adolph Hitler.

New Agers commonly teach that there is no absolute truth.[106] However, this is a self-refuting belief. If the belief that there is no absolute truth is true, then it would be an absolute truth (universally true). Therefore, it is self-refuting, and it must be false. Hence, some things must be universally true.

New Agers seek the establishment of a one-world government.[107] They believe that man himself will bring a new age of peace to the earth.[108] However, God wants the world divided into separate nations until Jesus returns to rule (Genesis 11:1-9). A man-made, one-world government may eventually lead to the global dictatorship headed by the antichrist (Revelation 13:3-7). The Bible teaches that there will be wars until the end, and that mankind will not be able to establish peace on earth by himself (Daniel 9:26; Matthew 24:6-7). Jesus taught that in the last days the love of man would grow cold (Matthew 24:12). Only Jesus, the true Prince of Peace, will be able to bring lasting peace to the planet (Isaiah 9:6-7; Revelation 11:15; 19:11-16). A one-world human government will only expedite man's self-destruction.

New Agers believe mankind is evolving and getting better. But, history agrees with the biblical depiction of man as eroding morally. In fact, this century has been the bloodiest century in human history. New Age optimism about the future is clearly unwarranted. Man is not getting better; he is getting worse.

New Agers often say that all religions lead to God.[109] Again, this contradicts the teaching of Scripture. Jesus taught that salvation comes only through faith in Him (John 3:16-18; 14:6; Acts 4:12). Jesus taught that those who reject Him do not have a saving relationship with God the Father (Luke 10:16). Thus, the Bible denies that all faiths lead to God.

New Agers deny that Jesus is uniquely God.[110] They deny that salvation comes only through Jesus and that man is lost without Him.[111] Obviously, the New Age Movement is not compatible with biblical Christianity.

Common New Age Practices. Two common New Age practices are channeling and eastern meditation.[112] Channeling is the practice whereby a person voluntarily allows himself to be possessed by a spiritual entity who then speaks through the possessed person. The spirit entity is thought to be the spirit of a deceased human.[113] The Bible forbids people to attempt to communicate with the dead (Deuteronomy 18:9-12; Isaiah 8:19). The Word of God also indicates that the dead cannot communicate with the living (Luke 16:19-31). Therefore, the spirit entities that possess and speak through people are probably demons; they are not spirits of dead humans. The Bible commands men and women to test the spirits (1 John 4:1-3). The apostle Paul predicts that in the last days men will fall prey to doctrines taught by demons (1 Timothy 4:1). The content of channeled messages contradicts the gospel message of salvation only through faith in Jesus.[114] Paul stated that any human or angel who brings a message that contradicts the gospel is accursed (Galatians 1:8-9).

New agers commonly practice eastern meditation.[115] Eastern meditation encourages a person to empty his mind of all rational thought. This is believed to create an environment in which a mystical union with the impersonal god can take place.[116] Eastern meditation differs essentially from biblical meditation. In biblical meditation, the person's mind is emptied of sinful desires. Still, the mind is focused on principles from God's Word (Psalm 1:1-2; Joshua 1:8). Therefore, in biblical meditation, the mind is never left completely empty. On the other hand, eastern meditation is content-less. One surrenders control of one's mind by the cessation of rational thought. Once a person loses control of his mind, demonic control may take place. Mantras are repeated during new age meditation.[117] A mantra is a one syllable word that, when repeated over and over, is designed to remove all content from the mind. This practice is in direct disobedience to the teaching of Christ. Jesus prohibited His followers from engaging in the vain repetition which was common among pagan worshippers (Matthew 6:7). The mantras have been shown to have been derived from the names of Hindu deities (false gods).[118] Therefore, eastern meditation invites demon possession through the communion with false gods (1 Corinthians 10:19-21), as well as through the surrendering of the mind.

The New Age Movement is not Christian. It competes with Christianity for the hearts of men and women. Therefore, defenders of the Christian Faith should follow the example of Walter Martin—we must be prepared to refute the doctrines of the New Age Movement.

CONCLUSION

The late Dr. Walter Martin was one of the greatest defenders of the faith in the twentieth century. In his day, he was the foremost expert on exposing and refuting non-Christian cults. His comparative religious apologetic methodology should not be ignored. There will always be pseudo-Christian religions that need to be confronted by Christian apologists.

Walter Martin saw the dangers that non-Christian cults presented to the church. He closed his book The Kingdom of the Cults by proposing five major projects for the church to embrace in order to battle the kingdom of the cults.[119] First, Martin argued for the need for careful research on the background and theology of each cult. The results of this research must be placed into the hands of pastors, missionaries, and lay people. Martin founded his Christian Research Institute in 1960 for this purpose.

Second, Martin suggested the use of computers to gather and disseminate information on the cults. We now see that this is a reality with literally thousands of apologetic and counter-cult websites on the internet.

Third, Martin called for the publishing of specialized literature (books, pamphlets, etc.) dealing with counter-cult research. This literature must be distributed to lay people as well as clergy.

Fourth, Martin called for a reevaluation of biblical education. He believed that Bible institutes, colleges, and seminaries needed courses and programs in apologetics and counter-cult research. He understood that church leaders needed to be trained in apologetics to the cults. He believed that a course in comparative religions or non-Christian cults should be a requirement for graduation at Bible colleges and seminaries.

And fifth, Martin suggested the sponsoring and promoting of counter-cult conferences. This would expose the church throughout America to counter-cult apologetics and ministries. Today, these conferences take place on a regular basis throughout America.

Though the evangelical church has come a long way in comparative religious apologetics since 1960, there is still a long way to go. Only time will tell if the church successfully fulfills the dream of Dr. Walter Martin, the original "Bible Answer Man."

ENDNOTES

1. Walter Martin, The Kingdom of the Cults (Minneapolis: Bethany House Publishers, 1985), 11.

2. Ibid.

3. Gordon B. Hinckley, Truth Restored (Salt Lake City: The Church of Jesus Christ of Latter-Day Saints, 1979), 1-30.

4. Ibid., 102-103.

5. Walter Martin, The Maze of Mormonism (Santa Ana: Vision House, 1978), 45.

6. Ibid., 48.

7. Ibid., 47.

8. Gleason L. Archer, Jr., Survey of Old Testament Introduction (Chicago: Moody Press, 1974), 509-512.

9Martin, The Maze of Mormonism, 59-69.

10. Ibid., 59.

11. Doctrines and Covenants (Salt Lake City: The Church of Jesus Christ of Latter-Day Saints, 1982).

12. Pearl of Great Price (Salt Lake City: The Church of Jesus Christ of Latter-Day Saints, 1982).

13. Josh McDowell and Don Stewart, Handbook of Today's Religions (San Bernardino: Here's Life Publishers, 1983), 68.

14. Bruce R. McConkie, Mormon Doctrine (Salt Lake City: Bookcraft, 1966), 576-577.

15. Ibid., 577.

16. Ibid., 238-239, 577.

17. Daniel H. Ludlow, ed. Latter-day Prophets Speak (Salt Lake City: Bookcraft, 71-79.

18. McConkie, 129.

19. Ibid., 669-672.

20. Ibid., 669.

21. Ludlow, 183-189.

22. McConkie, 72-73.

23. Ibid., 577-579.

24. Martin, Kingdom of the Cults, 38-46.

25. Mather and Nichols, 158.

26. Martin, Kingdom of the Cults, 47-48.

27. Mather and Nichols, 158.

28. New World Translation of the Holy Scriptures (Brooklyn: Watchtower Bible and Tract Society of New York, Inc., 1961), 1151.

29. Martin, Kingdom of the Cults, 71-83.

30. McDowell and Stewart, 47-49.

31. Let God be True (Brooklyn: Watchtower Bible and Tract Society, Inc., 1946), 34-35, 37, 88, 91.

32. Ibid., 89.

33. Reasoning from the Scriptures (Brooklyn: Watchtower Bible and Tract Society, Inc., 1989), 334-335.

34. Let God be True, 185-188.

35. Ibid., 189-192, 208-209.

36. Ibid., 297-301.

37. Ibid., 57-67.

38. Ibid., 68-80.

39. Ibid., 226-242.

40. Ibid., 21-32.

41. Ibid., 189-190.

42. Martin, Kingdom of the Cults, 133.

43. Mary Baker Eddy, Science and Health with Key to the Scriptures (Boston: The First Church of Christ, Scientist, 1971), 113, 115, 293, 336, 447, 468, 472, 480, 482, 584, 586, 587.

44. Ibid., 468.

45. Ibid., 473, 583.

46. Ibid., 588, 590, 593.

47. Ibid., 23-25, 45-46.

48. Martin, Kingdom of the Cults, 279.

49. Ibid., 284-286.

50. Ibid., 284-285.

51. Ibid., 286.

52. Ibid.

53. Ibid., 286-287.

54. Ibid., 338-339.

55. Walter Martin, Cults Reference Bible (Santa Ana: Vision House, 1981), 59.

56. Ibid., 59-60.

57. Ibid., 60.

58. Ibid.

59. Ibid., 59.

60. Ibid., 71.

61. Victor Paul Wierwille, Jesus Christ is not God (New Knoxville: The American Christian Press, 1975).

62. Martin, Cults Reference Bible, 78.

63. Mather and Nichols, 311.

64. Ibid., 251.

65. Ibid., 252.

66. Ibid., 253.

67. Martin, Kingdom of the Cults, 348-349.

68. Ibid., 501.

69. Ibid.

70. Mather and Nichols, 295.

71. Martin, Kingdom of the Cults, 501.

72. Mather and Nichols, 286-288.

73. Walter Martin, The New Age Cult (Minneapolis: Bethany House Publishers, 1989), 7-8.

74. Ibid.

75. Ibid., 13.

76. Ibid., 15.

77. Ibid., 33-34.

78. Douglas R. Groothuis, Unmasking the New Age (Downers Grove: Inter-Varsity Press, 1986), 116-117.

79. Miller, 202.

80. Ibid., 14-16.

81. Martin, The New Age Cult, 15.

82. Ibid., 15-17.

83. Ibid., 15.

84. Bob Larson, Larson's Book of Cults (Wheaton: Tyndale House Publishers, 1982), 327.

85. Martin, The New Age Cult, 15.

86. Ibid.

87. Ibid.

88. Ibid., 16-17.

89. Ibid., 17.

90. Ibid., 16.

91. Ibid., 129.

92. Geisler and Anderson, Origin Science, 82-83.

93. Groothuis, Unmasking the New Age, 37-56.

94. Ibid., 18-21.

95. Ibid., 20.

96. Ibid., 21-22.

97. Martin, The New Age Cult, 29-30.

98. Ibid.

99. Ibid., 32-33.

100. Norman L. Geisler and J. Yutaka Amano, The Reincarnation Sensation (Wheaton: Tyndale House Publishers, 1986), 28-30.

101. David K. Clark and Norman L. Geisler, Apologetics in the New Age (Grand Rapids: Baker Book House, 1990), 151-155.

102. Ibid., 71.

103. Martin, The New Age Cult, 65.

104. Ibid.

105. Miller, 107-111.

106. Douglas Groothuis, Confronting the New Age (Downers Grove: Inter-Varsity Press, 1988), 72-76.

107. Miller, 111-127.

108. Ibid.

109. Groothuis, Unmasking the New Age, 27-29.

110. Douglas Groothuis, Revealing the New Age Jesus (Downers Grove: Inter-Varsity Press, 1990), 17-21.

111. Ibid.

112. Miller, 36, 141.

113. Ibid., 141-142.

114. Ibid., 169-174.

115. Groothuis, Confronting the New Age, 23-24.

116. Ibid.

117. Miller, 94.

118. Ibid.

119. Martin, Kingdom of the Cults, 400-408.

CHAPTER SEVEN:

The Apologetic Methodology
of Blaise Pascal

....

Blaise Pascal (1623-1662) was a French mathematician and
scientist who is famous for his work dealing with the pressure of
liquids and the theory of probability. He also designed a calculating
machine, and, at the age of 16, wrote a book on Geometry which
caught the attention of the great mathematician, Rene Descartes.[1]

Pascal was a devout Roman Catholic who had a vibrant faith
in Jesus Christ.[2] Towards the end of his life, Pascal began to write
and gather notes for a book on Christian apologetics. Unfortunately,
Pascal died before he completed the project. A few years after his
death the notes were published in a book entitled Pensees, which
means "thoughts."[3]

Since Pascal did not himself complete his task on the Pensees,
readers must study Pascal's ideas and attempt to organize them in
as coherent a fashion as possible. Notable advancements have been
made in this area by Tom Morris[4] (formerly of Notre Dame) and
Peter Kreeft[5] of Boston College. In this chapter, I will attempt to
construct a basic outline of the apologetic methodology of Blaise
Pascal. I will also attempt to show the contemporary relevance of the
Pascalian method.

PASCAL'S VIEW OF REASON

Pascal was opposed to the use of traditional proofs for God's existence.
He wrote:

> The metaphysical proofs for the existence of God are
> so remote from human reasoning and so involved that
> they make little impact, and, even if they did help some

people, it would only be for the moment during which they watched the demonstration, because an hour later they would be afraid they had made a mistake.[6]

And this is why I shall not undertake here to prove by reasons from nature either the existence of God, or the Trinity or the immortality of the soul, or anything of that kind: not just because I should not feel competent to find in nature arguments which would convince hardened atheists, but also because such knowledge, without Christ, is useless and sterile. Even if someone were convinced that the proportions between numbers are immaterial, eternal truths, depending on a first truth in which they subsist, called God, I should not consider that he made much progress towards his salvation. The Christian's God does not consist merely of a God who is the author of mathematical truths and the order of the elements. That is the portion of the heathen and Epicureans.[7]

Pascal believed that even if these arguments for God's existence were valid, few would reason well enough to be persuaded by them. And, even if the arguments persuaded someone, that person would still not be saved. Pascal was concerned with leading people to Christ, not merely to monotheism (the belief in the existence of one God). Therefore, he believed the traditional arguments for God's existence were counterproductive.

Pascal was also opposed to the pure rationalism of Descartes. Pascal realized that there were more ways to find truth than through reason alone. Man could also find truth through his heart. By the heart, Pascal meant what we intuitively know as opposed to what we know through deductive reasoning.[8] We perceive and believe in God with our hearts. We will with our hearts.[9] We know first principles through the heart. Pascal not only recognized other ways of knowing besides reason, but he saw that man's reason is often influenced by other factors. Man is not always true to his reason. Pascal's view of reason can be seen in the following quotes:

We know the truth not only through our reason but also through our heart. It is through the latter that we know first principles, and reason, which has nothing to do with it, tries in vain to refute them. The skeptics have no other object than that, and they work at it to no purpose. We know that we are not dreaming, but, however unable we may be to prove it rationally, our inability proves nothing but the weakness of our reason, and not the uncertainty of all our knowledge, as they maintain. For knowledge of first principles, like space, time, motion, number, is as solid as any derived through reason, and it is on such knowledge, coming from the heart and instinct, that reason has to depend and base all its argument. . . It is just as pointless and absurd for reason to demand proof of first principles from the heart before agreeing to accept them as it would be absurd for the heart to demand an intuition of all the propositions demonstrated by reason before agreeing to accept them. Our inability must therefore serve only to humble reason, which would like to be judge of everything, but not to confute our certainty. As if reason were the only way we could learn![10]

The mind of this supreme judge of the world. . . Do not be surprised if his reasoning is not too sound at the moment, there is a fly buzzing round his ears; this is enough to render him incapable of giving good advice.[11]

Would you not say that this magistrate, whose venerable age commands universal respect, is ruled by pure, sublime reason, and judges things as they really are, without paying heed to the trivial circumstances which offend only the imagination of the weaker men? See him go to hear a sermon . . . If, when the preacher appears, it turns out that nature has given him a hoarse voice and an odd sort of face, that his barber has shaved him badly and he happens not to be too clean either, then, whatever great truths he may announce, I wager that our senator will not be able to keep a straight face. . . . Anyone who chose to follow reason alone would have proved himself a fool . . . Reason never wholly overcomes imagination, while the contrary is quite common.[12]

Be humble, impotent reason! Be silent, feeble nature! Learn that man infinitely transcends man, hear from your master your true condition, which is unknown to you. Listen to God.[13]

Descartes. . . we do not think that the whole of philosophy would be worth an hour's effort.[14]

The heart has its reasons of which reason knows nothing.[15]

It is the heart which perceives God and not the reason. That is what faith is: God perceived by the heart, not by the reason.[16]

It is important to note that Pascal is not an irrationalist. He recognizes that reason has its place; still, he reminds us that there are other ways of finding truth besides reason:

Two excesses: to exclude reason, to admit nothing but reason.[17]

Reason's last step is the recognition that there are an infinite number of things beyond it. It is merely feeble if it does not go as far as to realize that. If natural things are beyond it, what are we to say about supernatural things?[18]

130

If we submit everything to reason our religion will be left with nothing mysterious or supernatural.[19]

It is apparent that Pascal is not a fideist. He believed there was a place for reason in religious discussions. Still, he was not a pure rationalist. He differed from Descartes in that he did not believe that man could find all truth through reason alone; he did not believe man could deduce everything from from one point of rational certainty. Pascal respected the role of reason in knowing truth; but, he also recognized that reason has its limits.[20]

Pascal was willing, as we shall see, to use reason to defend the Christian Faith. Still, he recognized man to be more than a thinking machine. Man comes complete with prejudices, emotions, a will, and a vivid imagination. The whole man must be evangelized, not just his mind. According to Peter Kreeft, "Like Augustine, Pascal knows that the heart is deeper than the head, but like Augustine he does not cut off his own head, or so soften it up with relativism and subjectivism and 'open-mindedness' that his brains fall out."[21]

Before reason can get started certain things must be presupposed. However, unlike modern presuppositionalists, Pascal held that these first principles could be known with certainty through the intuition of the heart. The Cartesian attempt to prove everything by reason alone was totally futile from Pascal's perspective. First principles are self-evident truths recognized intuitively by the heart. They cannot be proven by reason; they must be assumed in order for a person to even begin to reason.

Pascal was a man before his time. He saw where Descartes' rationalism would lead man. When pure rationalism (which characterized much of modern philosophy) failed to produce the answers expected of it, it eventually collapsed into skepticism and irrationalism (post-modernism). This was due to the failure to recognize the limits of reason.

The time is now ripe for Pascalian apologetics. When pure rationalism is scorned (even if it should not be), Christian apologists must learn to speak to the hearts, as well as the minds, of men. And we can learn this art if we sit at the feet of Blaise Pascal.

PASCAL'S WAGER

In my estimation, the next step in the Pascalian apologetic is known as Pascal's wager. Some believe that Pascal's wager is the climax of Pascal's case for Christianity; but I believe this is mistaken. Pascal first tells his readers that we do not use our reason in an unbiased way. Then he uses his wager argument to show that the wise man will be biased for God's existence before looking at the evidence. After showing that humans do not use their reason in an unbiased manner, Pascal pleads with his readers to wager their lives on God:

> . . . let us say: 'Either God is or he is not.' But to which view shall we be inclined? Reason cannot decide this question. Infinite chaos separates us. At the far end of this infinite distance a coin is being spun which will come down heads or tails. How will you wager? Reason cannot make you choose either, reason cannot prove either wrong. . . Yes, but you must wager. There is no choice, you are already committed. Which will you choose then? . . . Let us weigh up the gain and the loss involved in calling heads that God exists. Let us assess the two cases: if you win you win everything, if you lose you lose nothing. Do not hesitate then; wager that he does exist. . . . And thus, since you are obliged to play, you must be renouncing reason if you hoard your life rather than risk it for an infinite gain, just as likely to occur as a loss amounting to nothing. . . . Thus our argument carries infinite weight, when the stakes are finite in a game where there are even chances of winning and losing and an infinite prize to be won.[22]

Pascal tells his readers that we must wager our lives on either God existing or God not existing. Reason, due to its limitations, cannot make the decision for us. We cannot avoid choosing sides; for, to not wager is equivalent with wagering against God.

If you wager on God, there are only two possible outcomes. If He exists, you win eternal life. If He does not exist, you lose nothing.

However, if you wager against God existing, there are also only two possible consequences. If He does not exist, you win nothing. But, if He does exist, you lose everything.

Therefore, since you have nothing to lose and everything to gain, the wise man will wager that God exists. Pascal is not trying to rationally prove God's existence with this argument. Instead, he is attempting to persuade the unbeliever that it wise to live as if God exists, while it is unwise to live as if God does not exist. Pascal believed that everyone who sincerely seeks God will find Him (Jeremiah 29:13).

Pascal attempts to show his readers that the wise man will be biased for God, not aginst God. He knew that human reason is limited and fallible, and that we do not use our reason in an unbiased manner. Through his wager argument, Pascal tries to convince his readers that, since we will use our reason in a biased manner, there are good reasons to be biased in favor of theism, and no reason to be biased for atheism.

The wager argument is Pascal's attempt to convince the nonbeliever to seek God. Pascal wrote:

> . . . there are only two classes of persons who can be called reasonable: those who serve God with all their heart because they know him and those who seek him with all their heart because they do not know him.[23]

Richard Creel illustrates the strength of Pascal's wager with the following words:

> It would not be irrational for me to continue to search a lake and its environs for a child that I concede, along with everyone else, has almost certainly drowned. If you ask me if I believe that the child has drowned, then I will say "yes"—but I will add that I hope that my belief is false and that I think that my continued efforts to find the child alive are justified by the great good that would obtain were I to succeed. . . . In conclusion, when God is thought of as infinitely perfect goodness, it seems consummately rational to hope that there is a

God and to live as though there is, as long as there is no conclusive proof that there is not.[24]

Once we recognize that we need to wager our lives on God, we are ready to examine the evidence for Christianity. It is at this point that Pascal discusses existential (i.e., psychological) and historical evidence for Christianity.

THE PARADOX OF MAN

Pascal believed that only the Christian religion rightly explained man's nature. Man is both wretched and great. Many religions recognize man's greatness, but fail to see man's wretchedness. The New Age movement is an example; man is God and sin is an illusion. Other religions accept man's wretchedness but ignore his greatness. Secular Humanists consider man to be an animal; Behaviorists view man as a machine. Only Christianity sees man for what he really is—man is both wretched and great.

Pascal concludes that the Christian doctrines of Creation and the Fall alone adequately explain the paradox of man. Pascal believed that man's greatness could be explained in the fact that man was created in God's image. And he argues that man would not understand his wretchedness unless he had some remembrance of a former greatness from which he had fallen. Pascal wrote:

> Man is only a reed, the weakest in nature, but he is a thinking reed. There is no need for the whole universe to take up arms to crush him: a vapour, a drop of water is enough to kill him. But even if the universe were to crush him, man would still be nobler than his slayer, because he knows that he is dying and the advantage the universe has over him. The universe knows none of this. Thus all our dignity consists in thought.[25]

> Man's greatness comes from knowing he is wretched: a tree does not know it is wretched. Thus it is wretched to know one is wretched, but there is a greatness in knowing one is wretched.[26]

All these examples of wretchedness prove his greatness. It is the wretchedness of a great lord, the wretchedness of a dispossessed king.[27]

Man's greatness and wretchedness are so evident that the true religion must necessarily teach us that there is in man some great principle of greatness and some great principle of wretchedness.[28]

Man is neither angel nor beast. . .[29]

There are in faith two equally constant truths. One is that man in the state of his creation, or in the state of grace, is exalted above the whole of nature, made like unto God and sharing in His divinity. The other is that in the state of corruption and sin he has fallen from that first state and has become like the beasts. . .[30]

For a religion to be true it must have known our nature; it must have known its greatness and smallness, and the reason for both. What other religion but Christianity has known this?[31]

The dilemma of man, that he is both great and wretched, is easy to document. The gap between animals and man is too great for evolution to adequately explain. No animal species will ever produce a Plato or Aristotle. Yet, the cruelty of man waged against man is unheard of in the animal kingdom. No animal species will ever produce a Hitler or Stalin.

Only Christianity with its doctrine of Creation and the Fall can adequately explain both aspects of man. Twentieth-century Christian apologists such as Francis Schaeffer[32] and Ravi Zacharias[33] continued the Pascalian tradition by using man's greatness and wretchedness as evidence for Christianity.

THE HUMAN CONDITION

Pascal sees the human condition as ultimately a one-way road to death. Death is a fact from which all men try to hide; nonetheless, it is a fact. We will all eventually die. . . and we know it. However, we live as if we will never die. The words of Pascal are haunting:

> Imagine a number of men in chains, all under sentence of death, some of whom are each day butchered in the sight of the others; those remaining see their own condition in that of their fellows, and looking at each other with grief and despair await their turn. This is an image of the human condition.[34]

> It is absurd of us to rely on the company of our fellows, as wretched and helpless as we are; they will not help us; we shall die alone.[35]

> The last act is bloody, however fine the rest of the play. They throw earth over your head and it is finished forever.[36]

> Let us ponder these things, and then say whether it is not beyond doubt that the only good thing in this life is the hope of another life. . .[37]

> We desire truth and find in ourselves nothing but uncertainty. We seek happiness and find only wretchedness and death.[38]

> God alone is man's true good. . .[39]

All men will die, and they know they will die. Yet, they do not all live lives of despair. Pascal explains how man copes despite his hopeless condition.

MAN'S RESPONSE TO HIS HOPELESS CONDITION

Pascal states that man responds to his hopeless condition in three ways: diversion, indifference, and self-deception. Rather than admit human wretchedness and death and look for a cure, we would rather ignore the human condition and lie to ourselves. Pascal wrote concerning diversion:

> Diversion. Being unable to cure death, wretchedness and ignorance, men have decided, in order to be happy, not to think about such things.[40]

> If our condition were truly happy we should not need to divert ourselves from thinking about it.[41]

> We run heedlessly into the abyss after putting something in front of us to stop us seeing it.[42]

> I can quite see that it makes a man happy to be diverted from contemplating his private miseries by making him care about nothing else but dancing well. . .[43]

Contemporary society has multitudes of diversions. Television, radio, computers, video games, the theater, sports events, and our careers are just a few of the many ways we can occupy ourselves so as to keep our focus off of our wretchedness and inevitable death. If the NFL went on strike this football season, would church attendance increase? We need to remind our fellow man that eternal matters are of more importance than the temporary pleasures of this life.

Recently, I saw a truck with a bumper sticker which read, "Everyone needs something to believe in. . . I believe I'll have another beer." Pascal was right; man diverts his attention through temporary pleasures to hide the truths he wishes to ignore.

Indifference is another way in which man avoids dealing with his coming death:

> The immortality of the soul is something of such vital importance to us, affecting us so deeply, that one must have lost all feeling not to care about knowing the facts of the matter. . . Thus the fact that there exist men who

are indifferent to the loss of their being and the peril of an eternity of wretchedness is against nature. With everything else they are quite different; they fear the most trifling things, foresee and feel them; and the same man who spends so many days and nights in fury and despair at losing some office or at some imaginary affront to his honour is the very one who knows that he is going to lose everything through death but feels neither anxiety nor emotion. It is a monstrous thing to see one and the same heart at once so sensitive to minor things and so strangely insensitive to the greatest.[44]

The roar of a crowd at the Super Bowl is deafening, but place that same crowd into a church, and there will be only silence. They are passionate about the outcome of a football game, but indifferent concerning the eternal things of God.

The unsaved man not only ignores the horror of his wretchedness and impending death through diversion and indifference. He also chooses to deceive himself and others in an attempt to hide from the truth:

Self-love. The nature of self-love and of this human self is to love only self and consider only self. . . it takes every care to hide its faults both from itself and others, and cannot bear to have them pointed out or noticed. . . For is it not true that we hate the truth and those who tell it to us, and we like them to be deceived to our advantage, and want to be esteemed by them as other than we actually are? . . . people are more wary of offending those whose friendship is most useful and enmity most dangerous. A prince can be the laughingstock of Europe and the only one to know nothing about it.[45]

Blaise Pascal saw that the use of reason alone would lead few, if any, to Christ. Pascal realized man is ruled more by his passions than by his reason. Therefore, his apologetic methodology focused on shaking men out of their indifference and removing their diversions.

His apologetic reminds men that eternal issues are of far greater worth than mere temporary ones. Pascal did not try to reason men into the kingdom; he attempted to sway men to desire Christianity to be true. He encouraged men to earnestly seek the God of the Bible. Modern society is based more on pleasures and desire than on reason. Therefore, Pascal's method of defending the faith has great potential in our day.

Pascal believed that abstract argumentation is not appealing to most people; he recognized that man would rather discuss the concrete things of everyday life. Therefore, Pascal started his apologetic where most people would feel comfortable—with the person himself. Then Pascal would attempt to take the person out of their comfort zone by revealing the hidden, unattractive truths (such as wretchedness, death, and self-deception) about the person. All this was done to reveal to the person the shallowness of this life and the need for the eternal things of God.

HISTORICAL EVIDENCES FOR THE CHRISTIAN FAITH

Pascal is not a classical apologist, for he rejects the traditional arguments for God's existence.[46] But, he is also not a fideist or a presuppositionalist,[47] for no fideist or true presuppositionalist would provide historical evidences for the Christian faith:

> Prophecies. If a single man had written a book foretelling the time and manner of Jesus' coming and Jesus had come in conformity with these prophecies, this would carry infinite weight. But there is much more here. There is a succession of men over a period of 4,000 years, coming consistently and invariably one after the other, to foretell the same coming; there is an entire people proclaiming it, existing for 4,000 years to testify in a body to the certainty they feel about it, from which they cannot be deflected by whatever threats and persecutions they may suffer. This is of a quite different order of importance.[48]

> Advantages of the Jewish people. . . This people is not

only of remarkable antiquity but has also lasted for a singularly long time, extending continuously from its origin to the present day. For whereas the peoples of Greece and Italy, of Sparta, Athens, Rome, and others who came so much later have perished so long ago, these still exist, despite the efforts of so many powerful kings who have tried a hundred times to wipe them out. . . They have always been preserved however, and their preservation was foretold. . .[49]

. . . Thus instead of concluding that there are no true miracles because there are so many false ones, we must on the contrary say that there certainly are true miracles since there are so many false ones, and that the false ones are only there because true ones exist.[50]

Proofs of Jesus Christ. The hypothesis that the Apostles were knaves is quite absurd. Follow it out to the end and imagine these twelve men meeting after Jesus' death and conspiring to say that he had risen from the dead. This means attacking all the powers that be. The human heart is singularly susceptible to fickleness, to change, to promises, to bribery. One of them had only to deny his story under these inducements, or still more because of possible imprisonment, tortures and death, and they would all have been lost. Follow that out.[51]

The Apostles were either deceived or deceivers. Either supposition is difficult, for it is not possible to imagine that a man has risen from the dead. While Jesus was with them he could sustain them, but afterwards, if he did not appear to them, who did make them act?[52]

Pascal was willing to use historical evidences as proof for the Christian faith. He viewed the prophecies that Jesus had fulfilled and the preservation of the Jewish people despite centuries of persecution as strong evidence for Christianity. Pascal considered miracles, especially Christ's resurrection from the dead, to be valuable ammunition for the arsenal of the apologist. Pascal did not tell unbelievers to "just believe." He gave them evidence for the truth of Christianity. Still, he refused to use reason alone; his apologetic attempted to reach the whole man, not just his mind. Since Pascal used historical evidences for Christianity's truth claims, he can be classified as an evidentialist (also called a "historical apologist"). However, the unique aspects of his apologetic system (i.e., his emphasis on the limitations of human reason, his wager argument, and his focus on the psychological makeup of man) merit the title of "Pascalian Apologetics" for his appraoch to defending the Christian faith.

CONCLUSION

Blaise Pascal had a unique apologetic methodology. He was not a classical apologist, for he denied that the traditional theistic proofs were sound or useful in the apologetic project.[53] He was not a fideist, for he defended the faith.[54] And, he was not a pure presuppositionalist, for he used pyschological and historical evidences to prove the truth of Christianity.[55] At best, Pascal's methodology could be classified as a unique combination of psychological apologetics and historical apologetics.[56] He was a psychological apologist, for he attempted to speak to the entire man, not just his intellect. But, he was also a historical apologist since he was willing to use historical data to provide evidence for Christianity.

Though I appreciate and utilize traditional arguments for God's existence, I believe that the apologetic methodology of Blaise Pascal should not be ignored. Pascal has much to offer the contemporary Christian apologist. Every apologist can benefit from examining Pascal's insight into man's fallen nature, his identification of the limitations of human reason, and his desire to convert people to Christianity, not merely monotheism. Studying Pascal's apologetic methodology, and incorporating aspects of it into our own apologetic ministry, can make our defense of the faith more effective.

Today, unfortunately, many people are not concerned about finding rational truth.[57] But, they are very concerned about their existential experience. Many people seek meaning in life; they also want their deepest desires to be satisfied. At the same time, many people are reluctant to admit their faults. Therefore, the Pascalian apologetic methodology has great potential for contemporary society, for Pascal forces us to look at ourselves in the mirror. He forces us to see ourselves as we are: wretched, miserable people who will all eventually die. Pascal then tugs at our hearts and declares to us that only in Jesus can life have meaning. Only in Jesus can we find satisfaction and forgiveness. Only in Jesus can death, our greatest enemy, be defeated.

Pascal beseeches contemporary man to wager his life on the God of the Bible. He calls us to seek God with all our being, for Pascal knows that if we seek Him with all our being, we will find Him. And if we find Him, we win eternity.

ENDNOTES

1. The World Book Encyclopedia (Chicago: World Book, Inc., 1985), vol. 15, "Blaise Pascal," by Phillip S. Jones, 167.

2. Thomas V. Morris, Making Sense of It All (Grand Rapids: William B. Eerdmans Publishing Company, 1992), 8.

3. Ibid., 10.

4. Ibid., entire book.

5. Peter Kreeft, Christianity for Modern Pagans (San Francisco: Ignatius Press, 1993), entire book.

6. Blaise Pascal, Pensees, trans. A. J. Krailsheimer, (London: Penguin Books, 1966), 190. (In this chapter, the number following any quote from the Pensees is the number of the Pensee, not the page number.)

7. Ibid., 449.

8. Kreeft, 228. See also Frederick Copleston, A History of Philosophy vol. IV (New York: Image Books, 1960), 166-167.

9. Kreeft, 228.

10. Pensees, 110.

11. Ibid., 48.

12. Ibid., 44.

13. Ibid., 131.

14. Ibid., 84.

15. Ibid., 423.

16. Ibid., 424.

17. Ibid., 183.

18. Ibid., 188.

19. Ibid., 173.

20. Morris, 183.

21. Kreeft, 235.

22. Pensees, 418.

23. Ibid., 427.

24. Richard E. Creel, "Agatheism: A Justification of the Rationality of Devotion to God," Faith and Philosophy, vol. 10 (January 1993): 40, 45.

25. Pensees, 200.

26. Ibid., 114.

27. Ibid., 116.

28. Ibid., 149.

29. Ibid., 678.

30. Ibid., 131.

31. Ibid., 215.

32. Francis A. Schaeffer, Trilogy (Wheaton: Crossway Books, 1990), 109-114.

33. Ravi Zacharias, Can Man Live Without God? (Dallas: Word Publishing, 1994), 133-145.

34. Pensees, 434.

35. Ibid., 151.

36. Ibid, 165.

37. Ibid., 427.

38. Ibid., 401.

39. Ibid., 148.

40. Ibid., 133.

41. Ibid., 70.

42. Ibid., 166.

43. Ibid., 137.

44. Ibid., 427.

45. Ibid., 978.

46. Classical apologists such as Anselm, Aquinas, Bonaventure, Paley, Norman Geisler, William Lane Craig, J. P. Moreland, and myself are willing to use philosophical and scientific arguments to provide evidence for God's existence. Pascal, on the other hand, considered traditional arguments for God's existence to be a waste of time. His wager argument is not technically an argument for God's existence; rather, it is an argument that a person ought to hope that God exists and live as if God exists. Boa and Bowman state, ". . . classical apologists maintain that at least one, and perhaps several, of the traditional arguments [for God's existence] are sound." See Kenneth D. Boa and Robert M. Bowman Jr., Faith Has Its Reasons—An Integrative Approach to Defending Christianity (Waynesboro, GA: Paternoster, 2005), 133. The distinguished apologist Norman Geisler states "Classical apologetics stresses rational arguments for the existence of God and historical evidence supporting the truth of Christianity. . . Classical apologetics is characterized by two basic steps. Its first step is to establish valid theistic arguments for the truth of theism apart from (but with appeal to) special revelation in Scripture. Its second step is to compile historical evidence to establish such basic truths of Christianity as the deity of Christ and the inspiration of the Bible." See Norman L. Geisler, Baker Encyclopedia of Christian Apologetics (Grand Rapids: Baker Book House, 1999), 154, 41-42. Pascal was disinterested in the first step of the classical apologetic methodology—he did not consider using traditional arguments for God's existence as a worthwhile endeavor. After pointing out the limitations of human reason, he pragmatically argues that we should wager our lives on God (i.e., desire that God exists and be open to evidence for Christianity in history). He then combines psychological apologetics with historical evidences (often called evidentialism) to make his case for Christianity. Though Pascal can be considered an evidentialist or a historical apologist (for he is willing to use historical evidences for Christianity), his apologetic methodology is so unique that it is probably best to refer to his methodology as "Pascalian." For descriptions of different types of apologetic methodologies see Boa and Bowman, 33-36, and Geisler, 41-44.

47. Fideists do not believe in providing any evidence for Christianity.

Presuppositionalists do not argue to the God of the Bible; rather they presuppose His existence and then argue from Him to certain aspects of human experience. Both fideists and presuppositionalists would not use historical evidences to argue for the truth claims of Christianity.

48. Pensees, 332.

49. Ibid., 451.

50. Ibid., 734.

51. Ibid., 310.

52. Ibid., 322.

53. Classical apologists utilize theistic proofs (i.e., arguments for God's existence). They first provide evidence for God's existence and then argue for the historical truth claims of Christianity. Classical apologists believe that the Holy Spirit will often use theistic arguments to chip away at the hardened hearts of nonbelievers, causing them to consider the reality of God's existence. In a second step, the classical apologist will usally turn to historical evidences for the truth claims of Christianity. See Geisler, 154, 41-42, and Boa and Bowman, 133. Contrary to classical apologists, Pascal did not believe arguing for the existence of God was a worhtwhile usage of time.

54. Fideists do not defend their faith; they believe that religious beliefs are to be accepted by faith, totally apart from rational evidences.

55. Presuppositionalists are not fideists—they are willing to defend the faith. Presuppositionalists are also not traditional apologists because they refuse to argue from something other than God to the existence of God. Presuppositionalists start with God— they presuppose the existence of the Triune God of the Bible—and then argue to common aspects of human experience (i.e., our moral experience, meaning in life, reason, etc.). The two greatest presuppositionalists of the twentieth century were Cornelius Van Til and Gordon Clark. An overview of their apologetic methodologies can be found in this work.

56. Gordon R. Lewis, Testing Christianity's Truth Claims (Lanham: University Press of America, 1990), 231-253. Lewis classifies Pascal's method as "psychological." Still, we must not overlook the stress Pascal also puts on historical evidences.

57. In the West, world views such as existentialism and postmodernism have led many people to deny the existence of absolute truth or man's ability to find truth through his reason. Eastern religions (i.e., Hinduism, Buddhism, etc.) de-emphasize or outright deny absolute truth. Many Americans have been influenced by these Western world views and/ or Eastern religions and consequently de-emphasize truth and reason, choosing to focus on the will, emotions, intuition, desires. Obviously, these people are greatly mistaken and they cannot live consistently with their world views. But, Pascal's psychological approach has great potential for aiding the Christian apologist in his attempt to reach people who are no longer interested in reason or truth.

ABOUT THE AUTHOR

....

Phil Fernandes is the senior pastor of Trinity Bible Fellowship and the founder and president of the Institute of Biblical Defense, an apologetics ministry which trains Christians in the defense of the faith. Both ministries are located in Bremerton, Washington.

Dr. Fernandes has earned a Ph.D. in philosophy of religion from Greenwich University, a Doctor of Theological Studies from Columbia Evangelical Seminary, and a Master of Arts in Religion from Liberty University. He has also earned a Master of Theology and a Bachelor of Theology from Columbia Evangelical Seminary. Fernandes is currently completing a Doctor of Ministry in Apologetics degree from Southern Evangelical Seminary. He has studied apologetics under leading apologists Gary Habermas and Norman Geisler.

He has lectured and debated in defense of Christianity on college campuses and in public schools. Dr. Fernandes has debated some of America's leading atheist voices (i.e., Michael Martin, Jeff Lowder, Dan Barker, Reggie Findley, Doug Krueger, and Robert Price). Dr. Fernandes currently teaches philosophy and apologetics for Columbia Evangelical Seminary and Crosspoint Academy. He is a member of the following professional societies: the Evangelical Theological Society, the Evangelical Philosophical Society, the International Society of Christian Apologetics, and the Society of Christian Philosophers.

Dr. Fernandes is the author of numerous books including: *The God Who Sits Enthroned: Evidence for God's Existence* (1997), *No Other Gods: A Defense of Biblical Christianity* (1998), *God, Government, and the Road to Tyranny: A Christian View of Government and Morality*

(2003), *Contend Earnestly for the Faith: A Survey of Christian Apologetics* (2008), *Evidence for Faith: Essays in Christian Apologetics* (2009), and *The Atheist Delusion: A Christian Response to Christopher Hitchens and Richard Dawkins* (2009).

Dr. Fernandes resides in Bremerton, Washington with his lovely wife Cathy. They have two grown daughters and three grandsons.

More than 1,000 audio lectures, sermons, and debates by Dr. Fernandes can be downloaded from the internet websites: instituteofbiblicaldefense.com and philfernandes.org. The Institute of Biblical Defense can be reached through the address or phone number listed below:

The Institute of Biblical Defense
P. O. Box 3264
Bremerton, WA. 98310

(360) 698-7382
tbf@sinclair.net